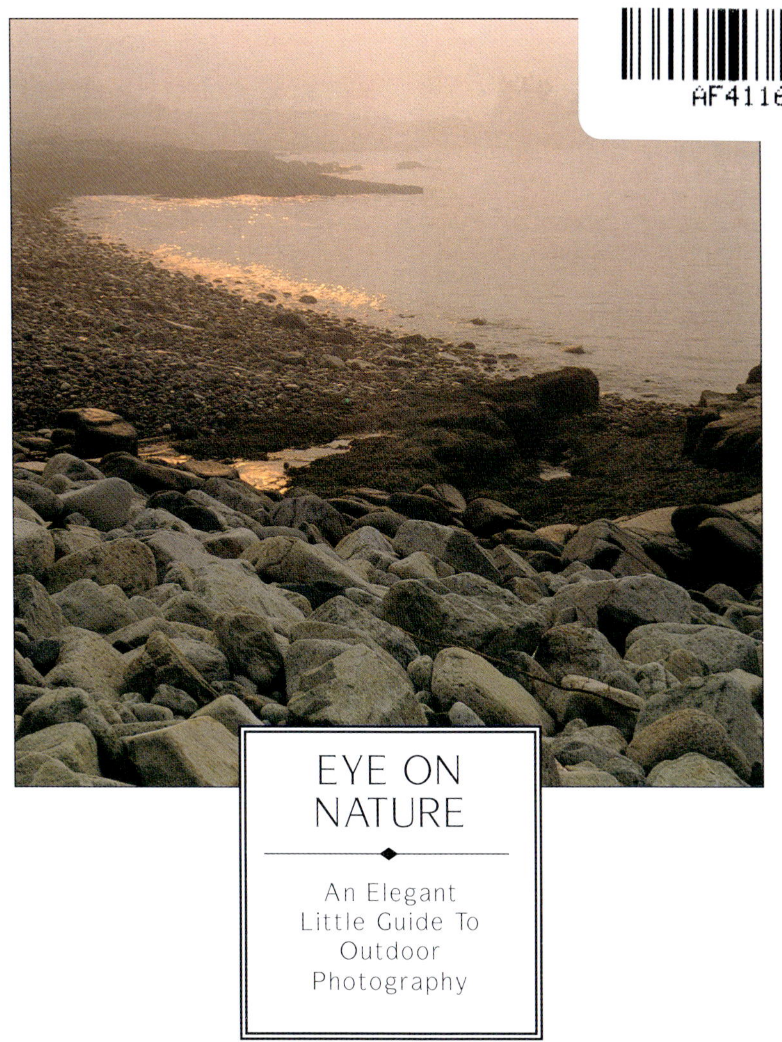

EYE ON NATURE

An Elegant
Little Guide To
Outdoor
Photography

Welcome to *Eye On Nature*, a guide to improving your outdoor photography and a collaboration between one of America's finest outdoor photographers and three companies known for their devotion to excellence in their products: L. L. Bean, Inc., Eastman Kodak Company, and Hasselblad USA.

In 1987, Judy Holmes decided to make the transition from corporate human resources director to professional photographer. Starting with programs at the Professional Photographers of America's Winona School, she tackled photography the same way she would any challenge in business, until she became one of the finest photographic instructors in the country. Perhaps it's Judy's business background that makes her approach to education, creativity and marketing unique.

We are very proud of our relationship with Judy and her persistent search for the ultimate outdoor image, camera, film and clothing. We hope you enjoy working with her over the next fifty pages as much as we have over the past several years.

Sincerely,

S. B. Cohen, President
Hasselblad USA Inc.

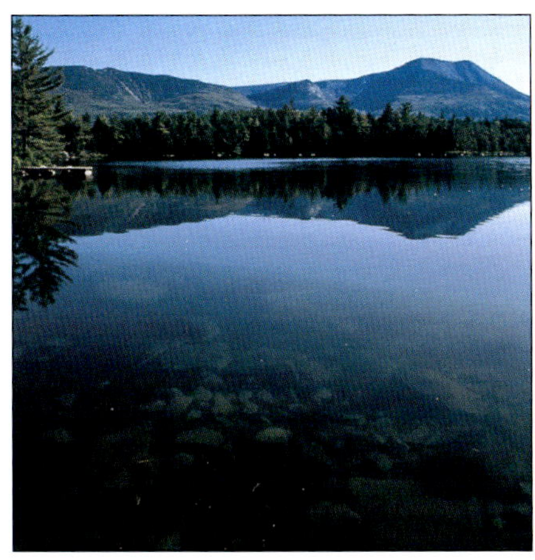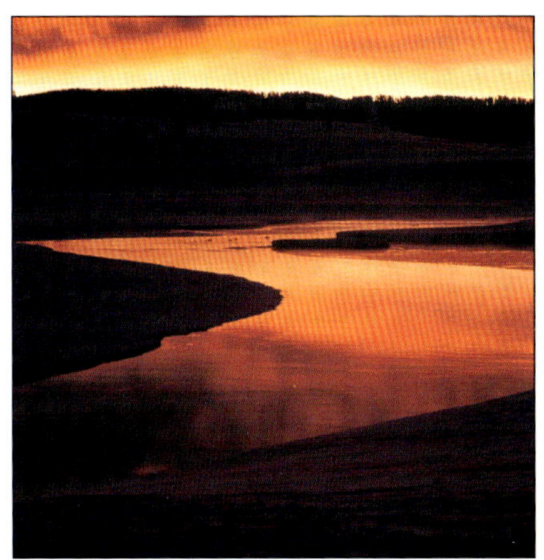

TABLE OF CONTENTS

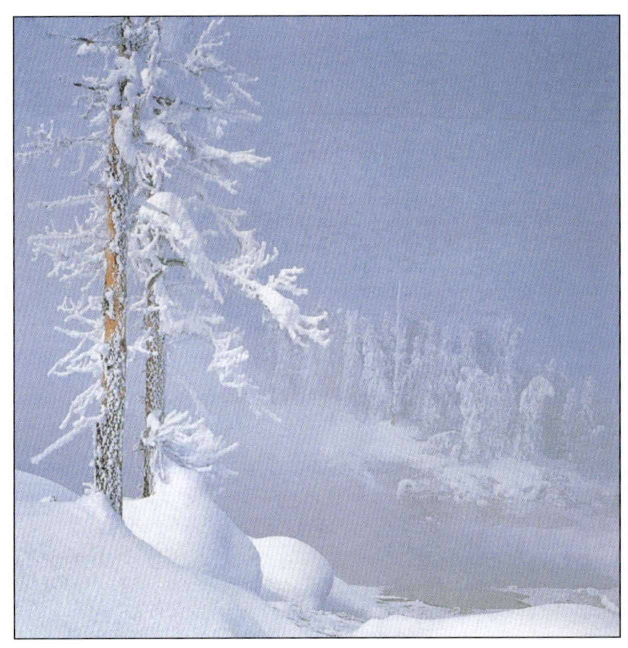

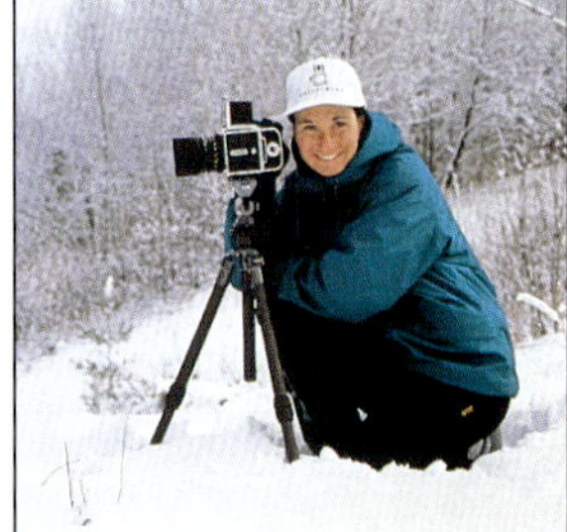

As the booklet's author and photographer, my goal is to provide you with techniques I've found useful in outdoor photography. The text consolidates information I've presented to thousands of amateur and professional photographers over the past few years. ■ I have tried to convey most of the message through the images, as the visual approach is my preferred way to learn. I'm often asked about equipment, film, and clothing. Here are my personal preferences - see if your style is similar and perhaps my selections will work for you. I hope so. ■ Enjoy wherever you are in your expertise and know you have a constant companion in your travels! I welcome your comments and questions. My address is on the inside back cover.

he L. L. Bean products you'll read about are my staples. Some of the fabrics and designs change as technology improves, but these are only modifications. It's a little like Maslow's hierarchy of needs – if I'm not warm, dry and well fed outdoors, I can't concentrate on the next level – my photography – at all. How I dress and pack has a lot to do with that comfort. Suggestions for clothing and travel items begin on page 48. Outdoor enthusiasts should request the Spring Sporting or Winter Sports catalog by calling 1·800·221·4221.

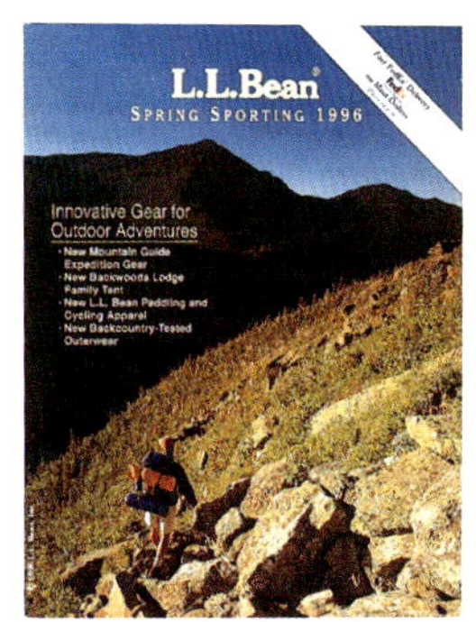

ou'll see how simple I keep my outdoor work. It starts with Kodak E100S, Pro 100 and 400, and T-MAX professional films. I rely on the consistency and variety of these 'home grown' products because they record the scene the way I saw it and because of the customer service Kodak provides to amateurs and professionals alike. See page 52 in the Sources section for their telephone hotlines for professional products and processing. Then use them! My film choices are on pages 46 and 47.

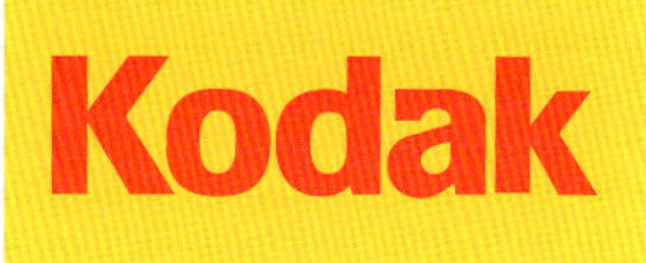

eople ask how, at 118 pounds, I can carry medium format equipment outdoors. It's not that heavy! Every piece I have works as well now as it did the day I purchased it, and I appreciate its nonobsolescence and reliability. Hasselblad offers three battery-free cameras in addition to its line of technically advanced electronic bodies, plus fifteen superb leaf shutter lenses, five film magazines, three formats, and almost two hundred accessories. Add to that the interchangeability of the film backs and you have an unbeatable system. See pages 42 to 45.

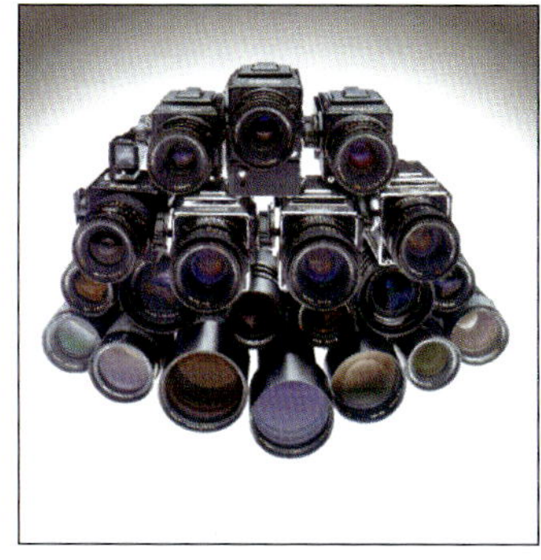

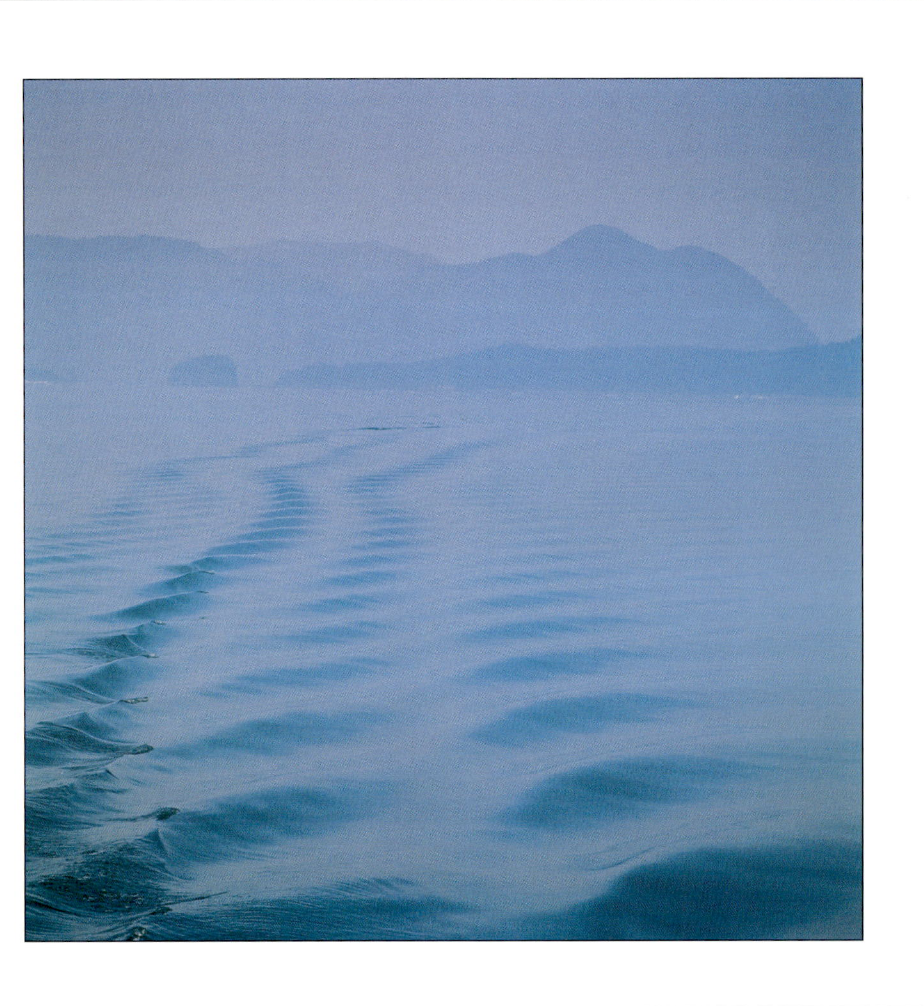

Anorak A jacket without a full zipper down the front – usually put on over your head. **Cold Weather Boots** Rubber-soled boots with thick felt liners and lace closures. I'm wearing them on page 50. Comfort rated to -10° F in active use. **Coolmax**® Polyester fabric that feels and wears like cotton, but transfers moisture away from the body. **Dark Slide** Flat stainless steel slide to keep stray light from entering the film magazine. Must be removed to release the shutter. **EV** Exposure Value – A number representing all those combinations of shutter speeds & apertures allowing the same amount of light to reach the film. 1/125 @ f/16 is the same value as 1/250 @ f/11, e.g. **Fleece** A soft polyester fabric made into layering garments from shirt weight (microfleece) to light, medium, and heavy jacket weights. Stows easily, dries quickly. **Gaiters** Provide foot protection from snow, rain, mud. Fit over boot and snug leg just below the knee. I use them as a spare 'pocket' for an extra film back or accessory. **Gore-Tex**® A waterproof, windproof membrane made famous by W.L.Gore Assoc. Often sandwiched between a lining and outer layer – rain stays out and sweat escapes. **Light Disk** A round, compact, flexible circle of varying sizes and colors, used to brighten shadow areas or even out high contrast subjects. **Gray Card** A card of 18% reflectance to which the in-camera meter is calibrated. If a scene reflects more or less than 18%, place a gray card in front of the lens so that nothing else is visible, then take a meter reading. **Neutral Density Filter** Either 'graduated' or a specific density throughout. Cuts the light reaching the film. The graduated style is often used to tone down a bright sky so there are fewer stops of light difference between sky and foreground. **Open up/Close down** Refers to aperture – open up to widen aperture toward lower numbers (such as f/2.8 or f/4); close down to make aperture smaller (f/22 and f/32). **Overmitts** Waterproof/windproof mittens to wear over gloves in cold weather. A useful place for keeping a light meter or extra roll of film warm. **Polypropylene or Polyester** Synthetic fabrics appreciated for their wicking properties, moving wetness away from the skin. Often used to create high performance long underwear, liner socks and gloves. **Primaloft**™ Warm, packable, lightweight 'synthetic down' insulation. Versatile, indispensible, and dries fast: I layer it over fleece and under Gore-Tex®.

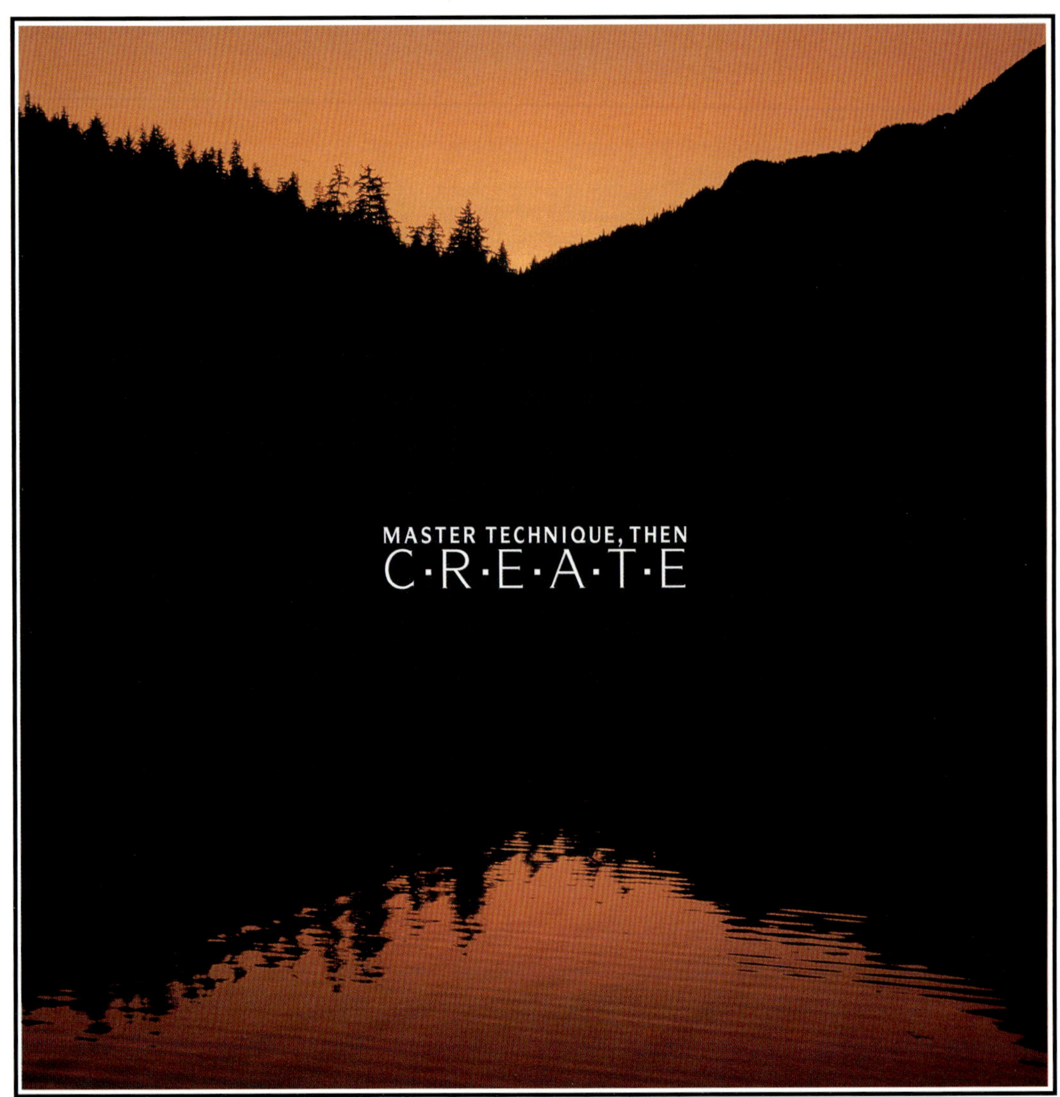
MASTER TECHNIQUE, THEN
C·R·E·A·T·E

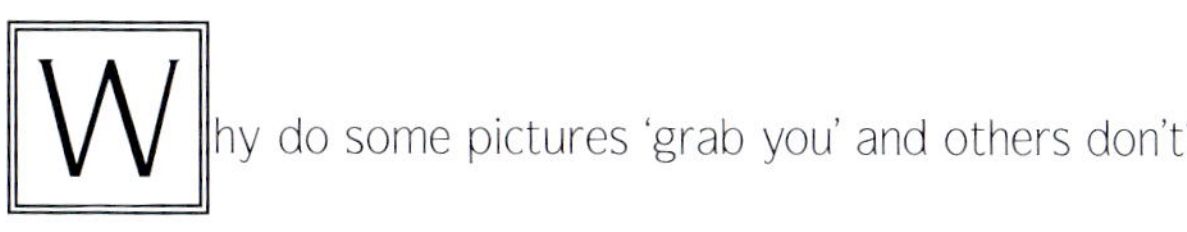

W hy do some pictures 'grab you' and others don't?

Like interesting architecture, advertisements, and clothes – certain principles are understood,

then manipulated to produce a unique statement. First, then, are elements to consider as you develop

your distinctive photographic style, followed by five steps to more expressive images. The result: you'll

begin defining a natural personality only yours. On a plateau? Happens to all of us after the steep

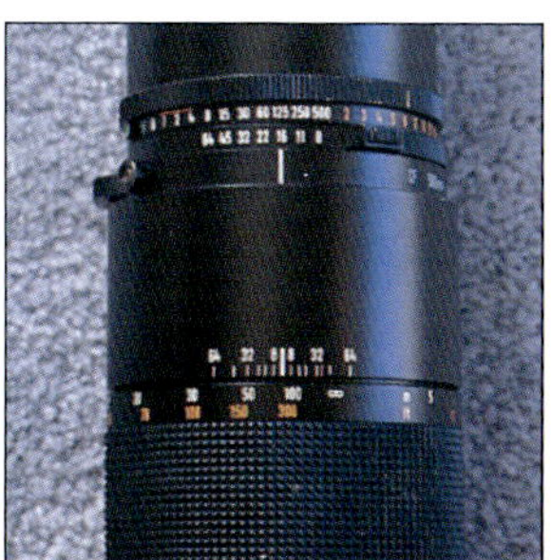

learning curve is conquered. See pages 32-35 for ideas to move

you off it. First, here's what a sunny day exposure with ISO 100 film

looks like on your lens barrel. This is an Exposure Value of 15. See p. 7.

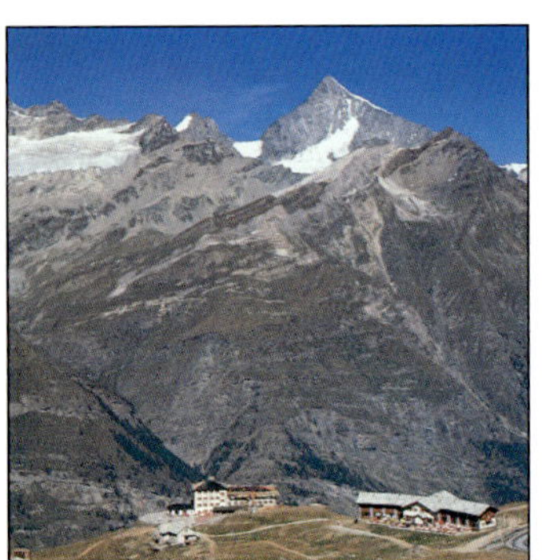

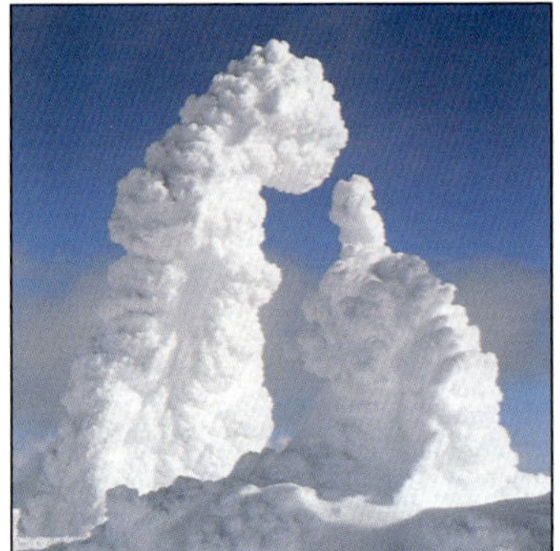

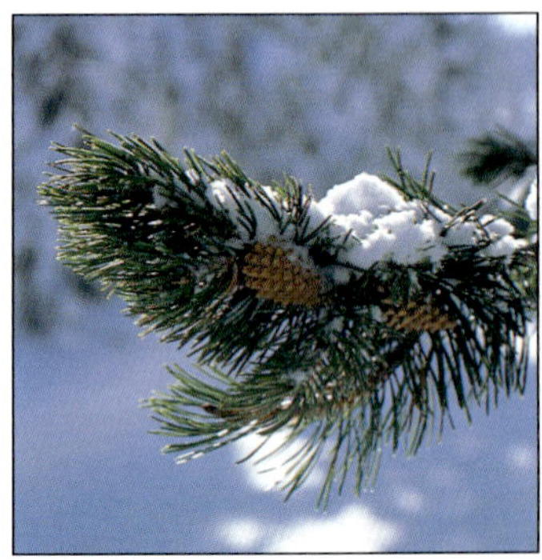

I train my eye as the first judge of light, then use a meter as second opinion. On a front-lit sunny day, 100 ISO film, any lens, no filters or tubes - set the lens at 1/ISO at f/16. This is Basic Daylight Exposure (BDE), inside back cover. (EV 15 on Hasselblad's lens barrel.) This is your frame of reference.

Add a stop of exposure time if the subject is side lit, rim lit, or the scene's a bit hazy or very bright overcast. This is EV 14, or 1/125 @ f/11, with 100 speed film. Learning to judge light based on a sunny day will mean getting a quick unmetered photo when you might have missed the fleeting moment altogether.

Add another stop of exposure for back lit or heavier overcast. Practice noticing small changes in light - soon you'll say "I think we just lost half a stop" or "This is an EV of 13, don't you think?" The result: you're in position to use any type of meter more intelligently.

Other Unmetered Situations

A silhouette requires less exposure time than a sunny day, by two stops. Either close down the aperture by two,

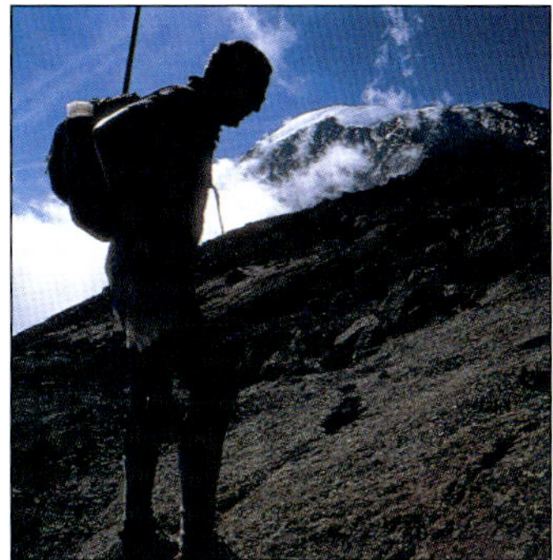

from f/16 to 32 at 1/125, or quicken the shutter by two stops, from 1/125 to 1/500 at f/16. This is EV 17 with ISO 100.

Situation: Sky retains luminescence but isn't a light source *or* brightly lit street scene retains detail, contrast when viewing through camera. Guide: "Rule of Ones": ISO 100 film @ f/11 for 1 minute. Lens at B, mirror up, hold gray card in front, release

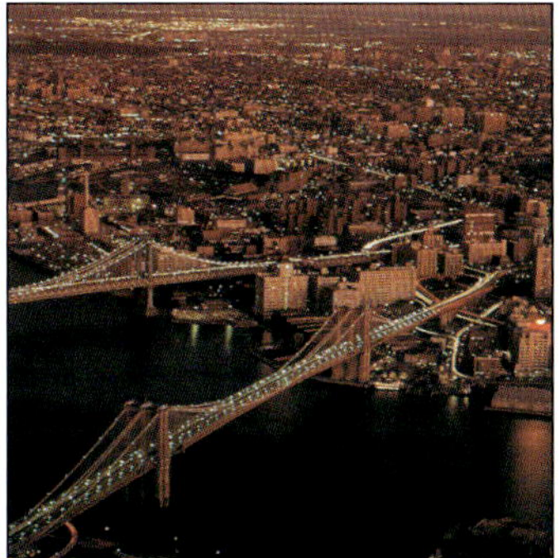

shutter, remove card, time exposure, replace card, unlock cable release. Experiment.

Scenes with black backgrounds allow great flexibility. For fireworks, lightning, or night skiers, I leave the shutter open for 8–15 seconds or as long as there's something interesting happening. The aperture? I prefer f/11 for lens sharpness, excellent contrast and reduced flare. But f/8 and f/16 work well too.

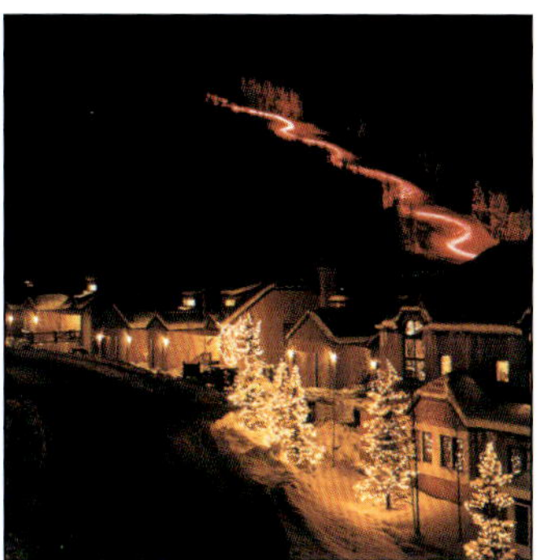

Meters And Their Strengths

The *in-camera reflected meter* measures light bouncing off the scene – if the elements present an 'average' tone, then the meter makes a reasonable suggestion. It has trouble with either very high contrast or very low contrast scenes.

A *reflected spot meter* is useful for taking several readings in a scene – if the range of light exceeds the five stops slide film can handle, you can decide what to highlight. Here, the sky, no sun, gave me an EV of 14 and the foreground an EV9.

For either high or low contrast scenes, the *incident* gives a true reading, provided you are in the same light. By measuring the light falling *on* your subjects, all are recorded accurately,

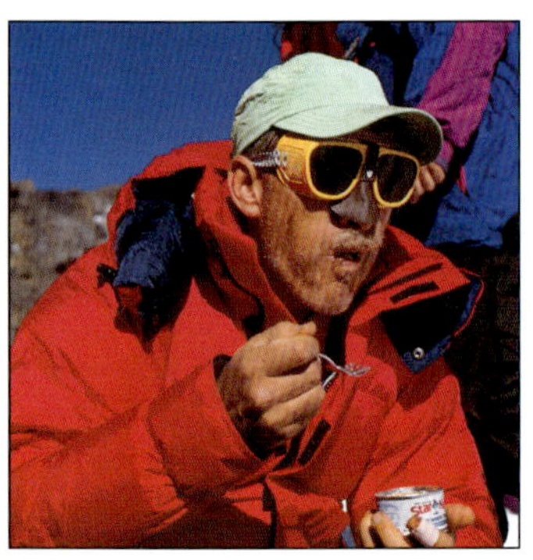

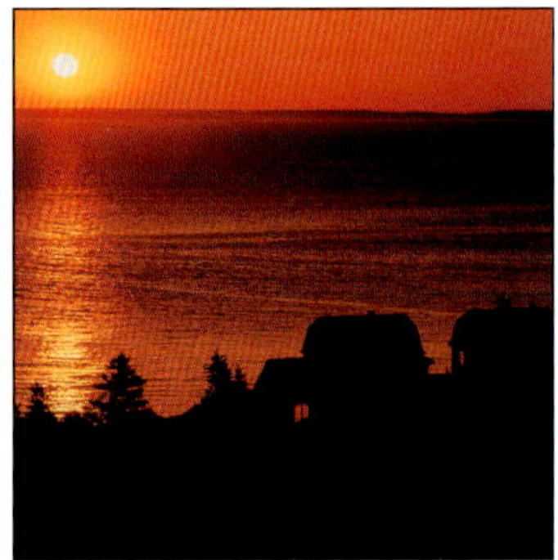

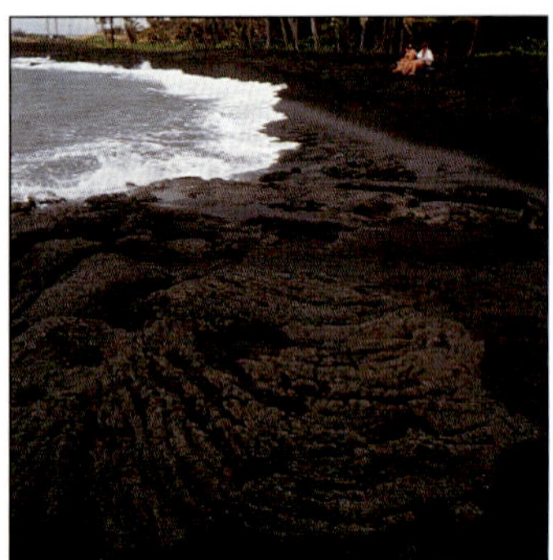

I went with the EV14, using 1/125 @ f/11, knowing the cemetery with sea gulls in front would go black.

regardless of their color or reflectance value. Thanks, Ernst Wildi, for one of my most important lessons.

Special Situations With Your In-Camera Meter For closeups, your in-camera meter takes into account the tubes, bellows, or other light-eating attachments you've added. But

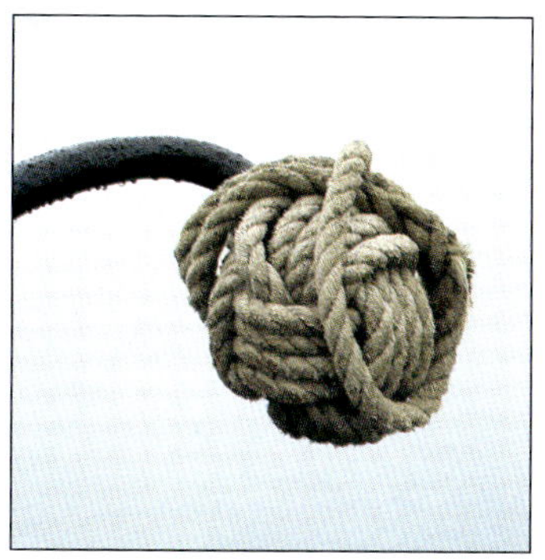

it still has trouble with high or low contrast scenes. So focus first, then insert a gray card between the subject and lens and take a reading.

There are two ways to correct a scene with too much contrast - either add fill flash (page 16) to brighten the shadows - or calm the highlights by shad-

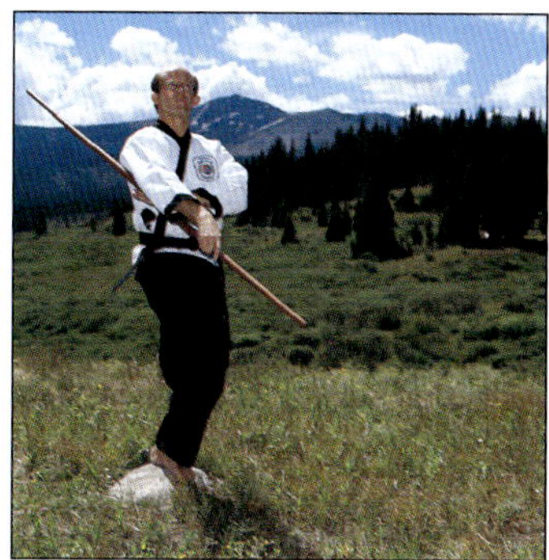

ing the subject, if small enough. This is 1/125 at f/16 - a sunny day exposure with ISO 100 film. I used fill flash, set at f/8, to light Buzz's shaded face. Adds some punch, not too much.

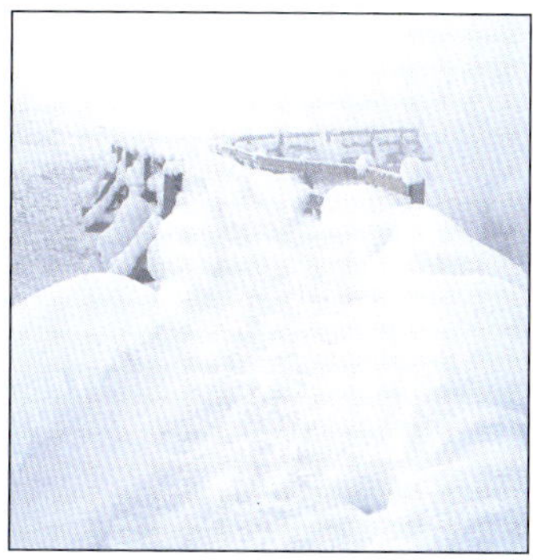

The meter says there's so much light present it will under-expose this scene. Either insert a gray card and use that reading, meter off your hand and open up a stop, or read off a medium tone in your clothing or camera bag. I gave this two full stops more exposure than the reflected meter indicated.

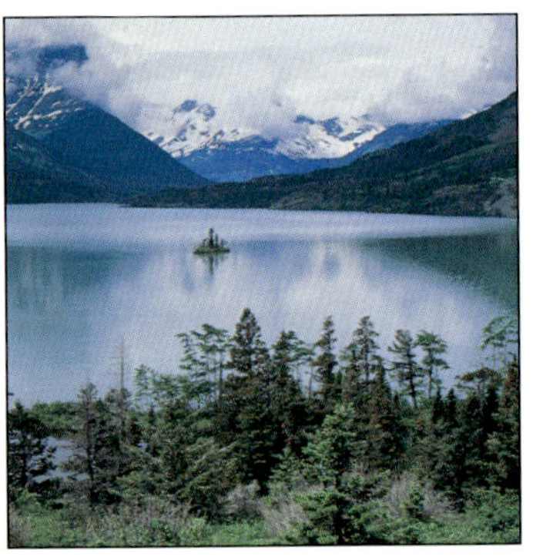

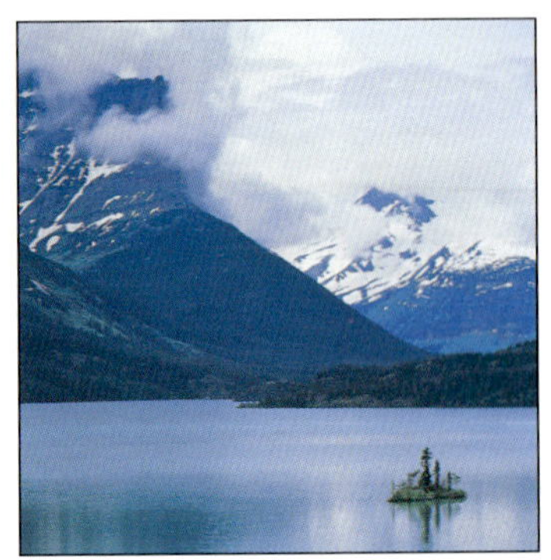

Bullseye! Great for darts, not so effective for scenics. Pretend the frame's a tic-tac-toe board and move the subject from small-center to larger-lower third. The interest is the island with the mountains behind it - so choose a longer lens and reposition the island. End result: more said with less clutter.

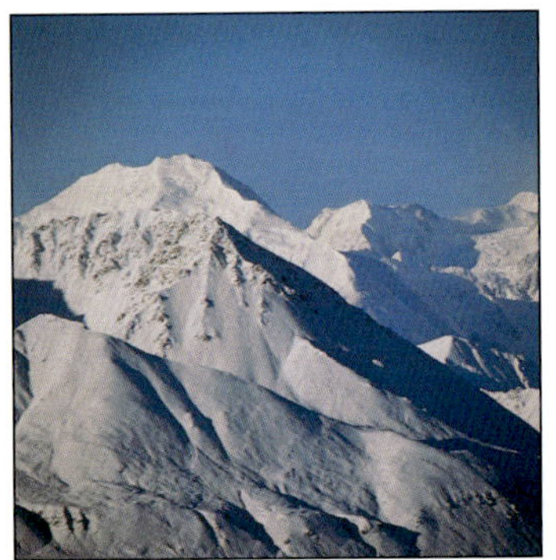

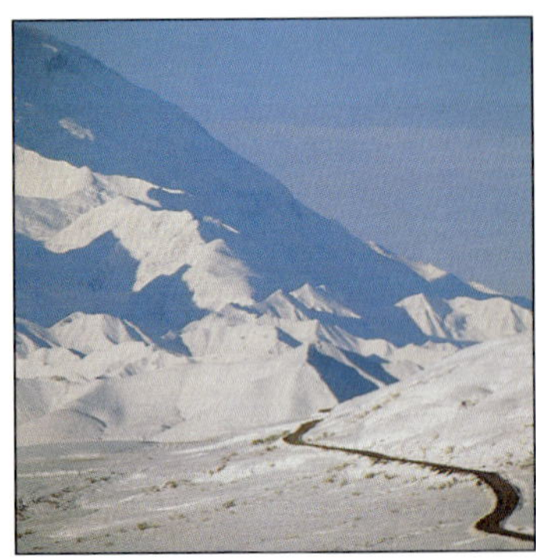

Majestic? Hardly. This looks more like a large landfill than 20,000+ foot Mt. McKinley. My pet peeve is leaving empty space above dramatic peaks. Look to your right - no comparison.

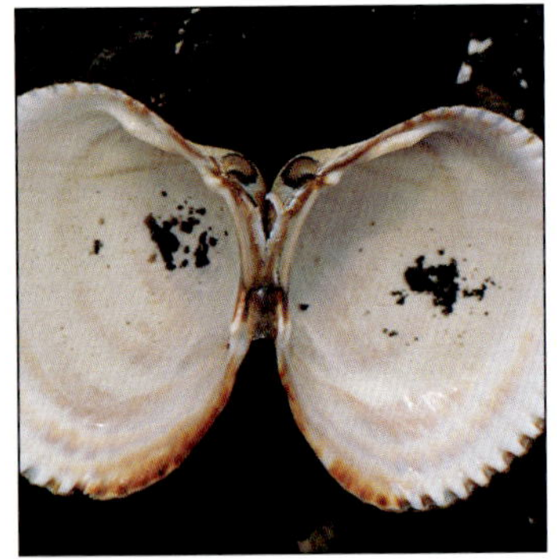

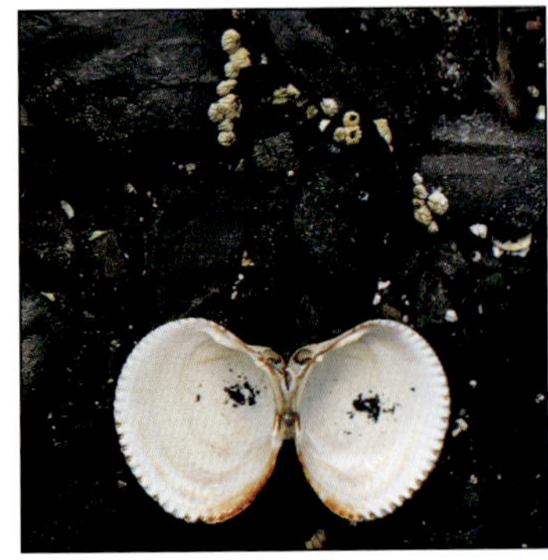

Ho Hum. Yes, it's close, even quite sharp. But so what? This bores me. Where *was* this cockle? How does the black play off the white? Close and sharp without purpose only proves you can focus the lens.

Pow!   Now break the rules or bend them. Since I want your eye to zero in on this spring trillium in New Hampshire, I'll fill the center of the frame with it. This will draw your eye in to the colors, shapes, and form of the flower.

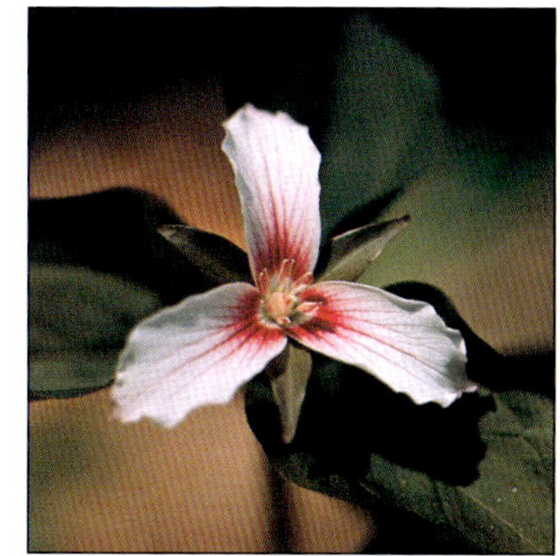

Out of Here!   Add vigor to an image by positioning a mountain as a backdrop. The range's stature isn't diminished by extending it out of the frame, it's just playing a supporting role by setting the mood on this misty morning at Wonder Lake in Denali National Park, Alaska.

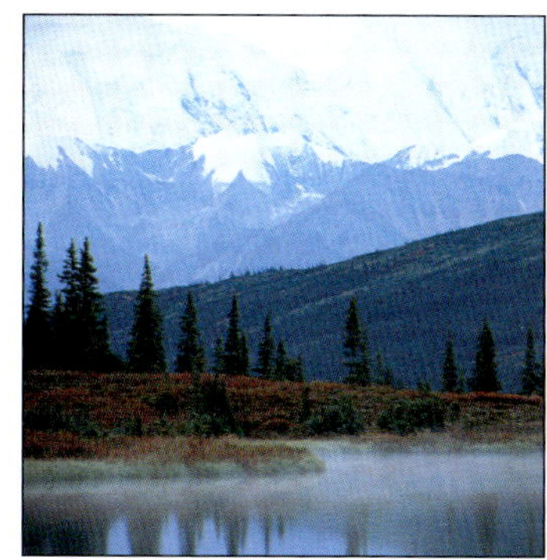

The Beach and Beyond!   The documented image pleases, but ask, "What else is in my bag to express this expanse of shore and sea?" The 30mm fisheye gives a perspective we can only dream about. See it low, see it high, see it like your lenses.

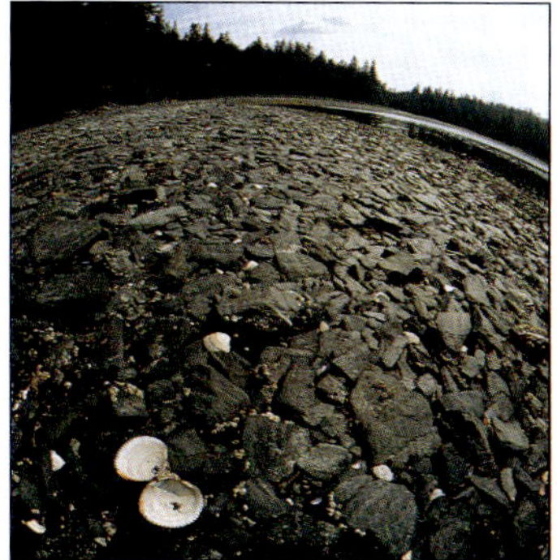

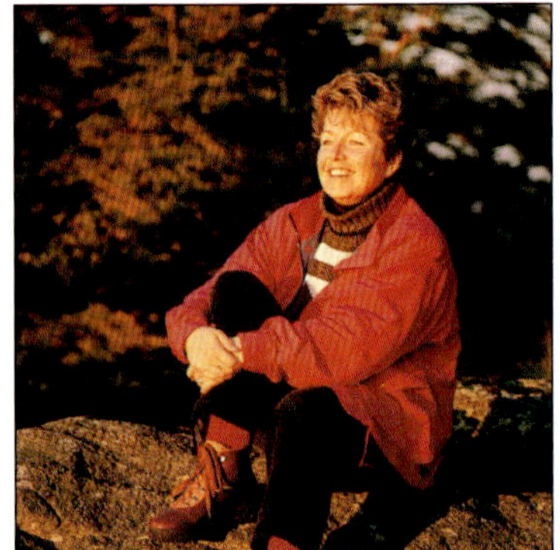

People and animals present some special considerations. I prefer photographing friends and animals in natural light whenever I can, and I like the face and especially the eye to be in focus and to sparkle. That's the first place your eye goes. The badger images demonstrate the importance of catchlight in the eye. If there isn't enough ambient light to make that highlight, I add fill flash. Since the flash isn't the main light source, take a meter reading as though you were exposing without it. Set the shutter for a speed that will stop the action, then set the aperture. If the correct exposure is an EV of 12, for example, try a shutter speed of 1/125, which means an aperture of 5.6. (The flash only cares about the aperture.) For a lot of fill, set the flash to one stop 'down' from the aperture, such as 4.0, or -1. For less fill, try -2. So much for the mystery of flash! See pages 13 and 29 for more tricks of the trade.

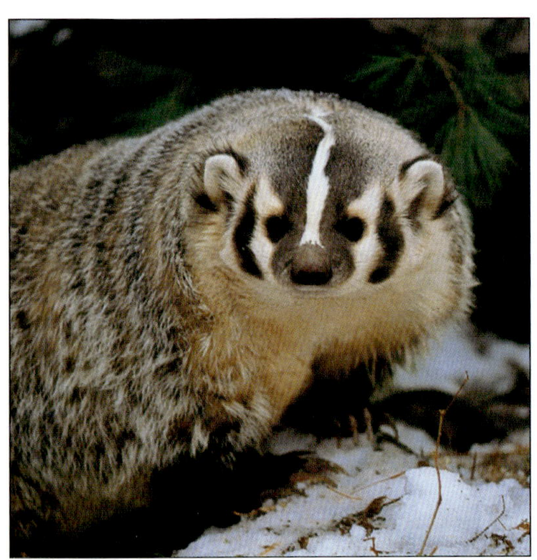

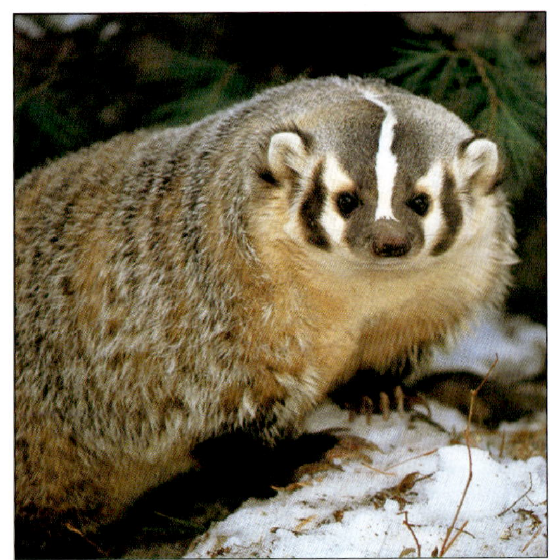

Animals 'pose' different considerations from landscapes. Whether the subject is photographed in the wild or in captivity, seek a natural position and use the film best suited for your final product (see pages 46 and 47). Choose the longest practical lens to avoid disturbing the animal. No image is *ever* worth that.

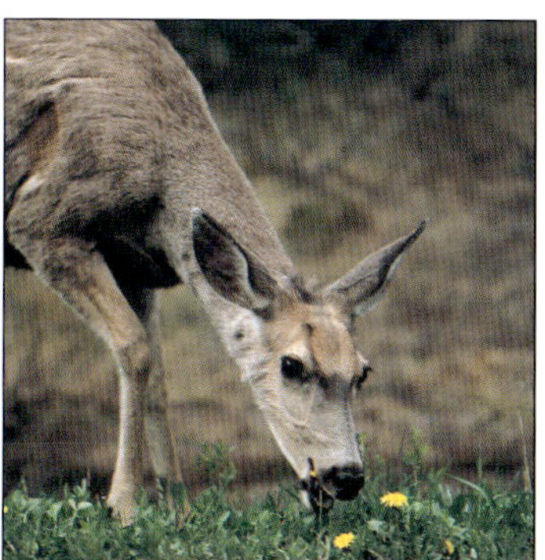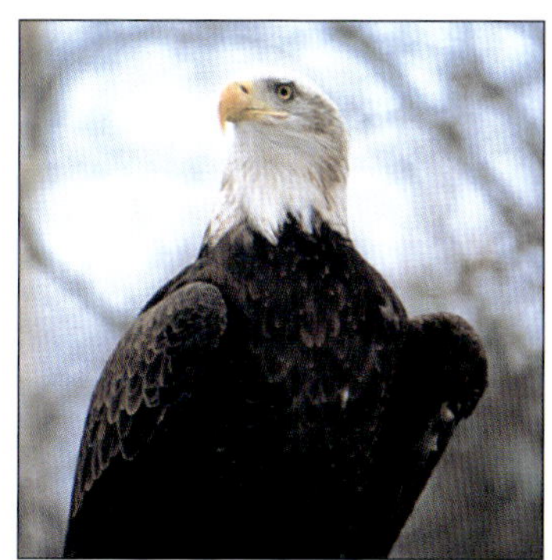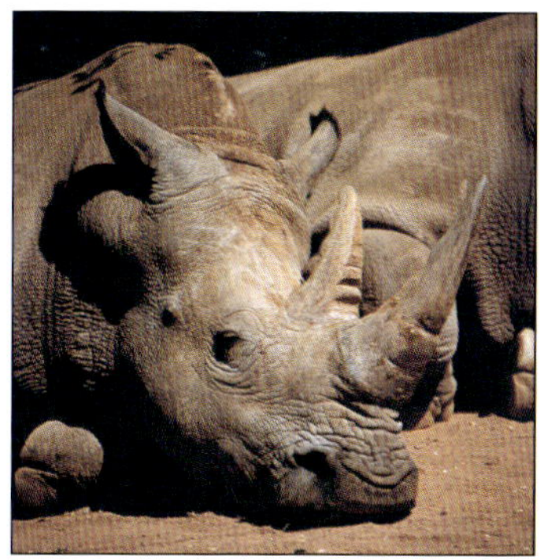

This deer munched dandelions as I photographed it in Waterton Lakes National Park, the Canadian neighbor of Glacier National Park in Montana. Besides showing the animal in the "wild," this view explains to school kids what the deer eats to survive. ■ Injured birds provide great subjects for two reasons – the $75 or $100 I spend to photograph them helps pay their rehabilitation, and they often sit perfectly still for portraits. Educational programs give people of all ages a chance to admire and appreciate wildlife. When photographing birds of prey, use a low camera angle to emphasize their stature. ■ A two-week trip to Africa may produce fewer images of rhinos than an hour in the local zoo! Tightly frame the animal with a long lens and aim through the bars to avoid showing barriers. My plea: don't hesitate to divulge your locale – a beautiful picture is a treasure. Period.

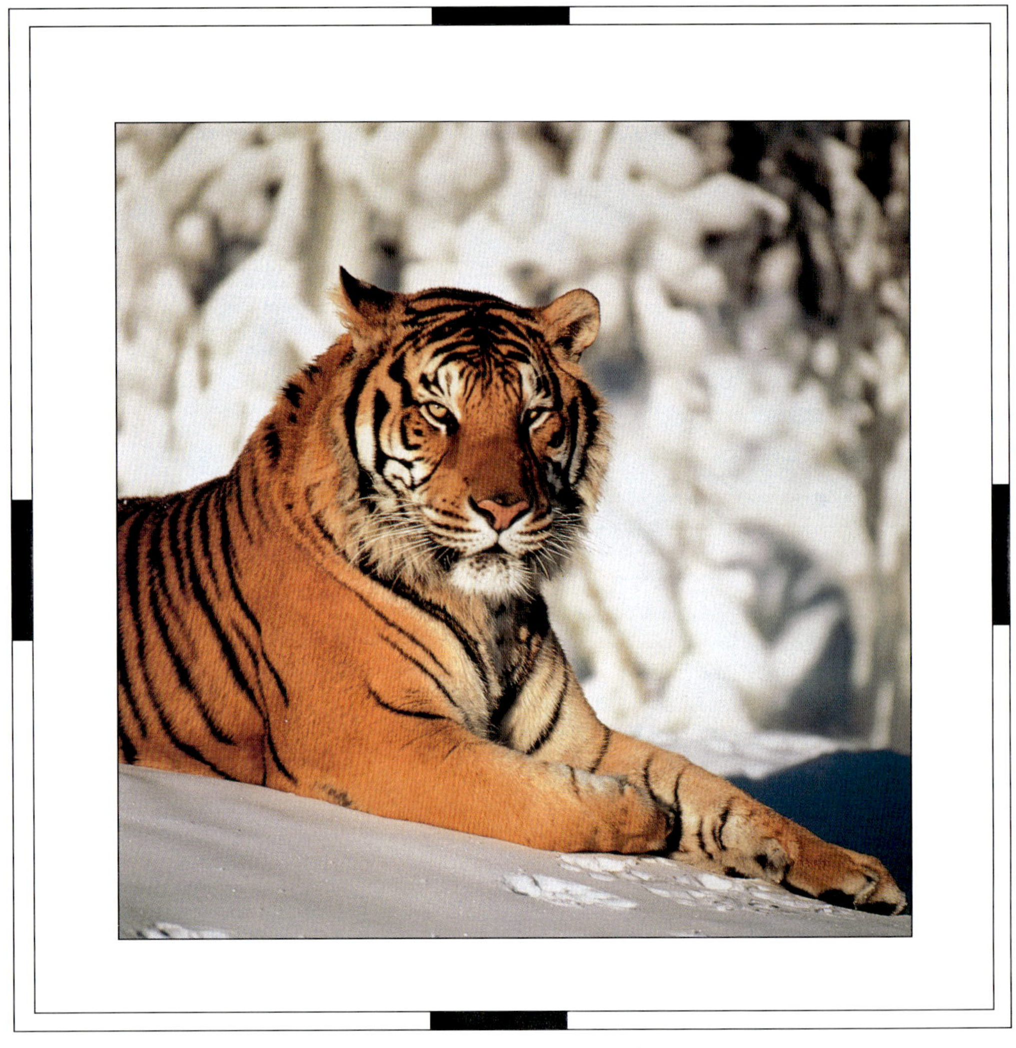

S eek good light (or improve it). Of the four kinds of light I identify in outdoor photography, only one is unpleasant all the time. I call it 'useless' light because the images I produce with it are just that. It is usually high noon, uneven and dead.

Early morning and late afternoon light, however, can make a mediocre photographer look good. But even high-contrast situations can be managed: I shade small subjects to provide uniform light when harsh shadows exist. Or I use fill flash. Cloudy days & rainy/snowy ones add an emotional aura not otherwise found. Equipment needs only

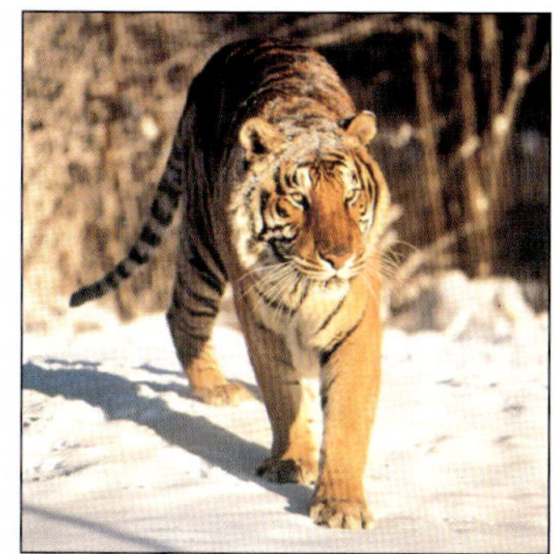

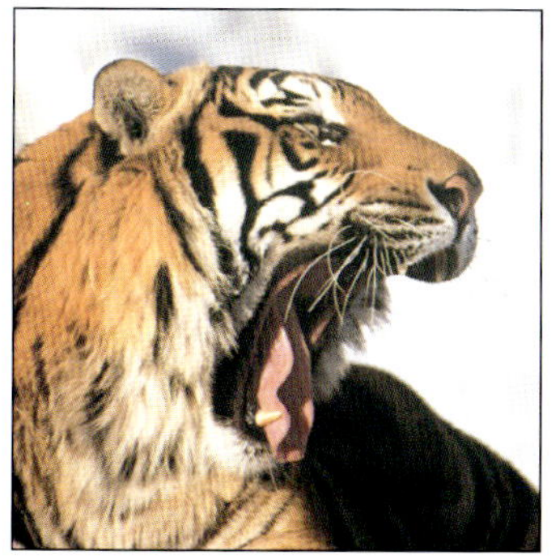

▲ Warm ▼ Bright

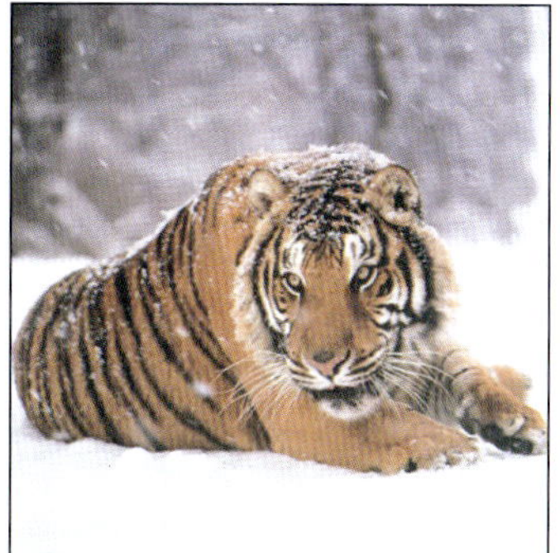

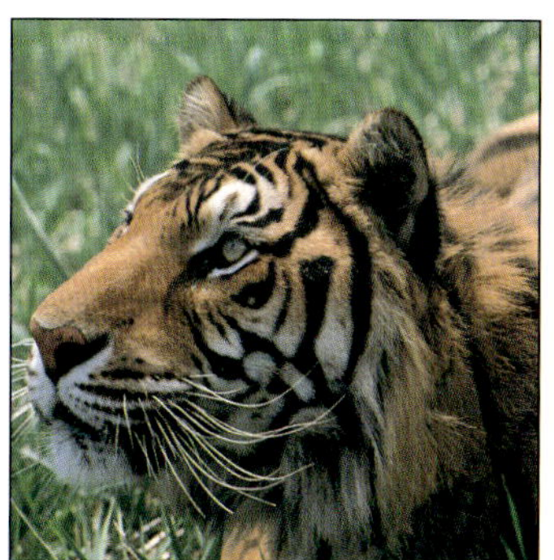

▲ Even ▼ Useless

a disposable shower cap or trash bag for protection along with a nylon lens wipe for maintenance. To avoid snow looking like large white spots or streaking across the frame, try a shutter speed of 1/30th of a second. The aperture will depend on how much light falls on the scene.

Are unusual conditions so special because many people don't want to photograph in them? On vacation, I often find fate has allowed the photographer a wonderful break - many family members sleep in during sunrise, stay indoors in wet weather, and return to the hotel at dusk. Is this good fortune for us or what?

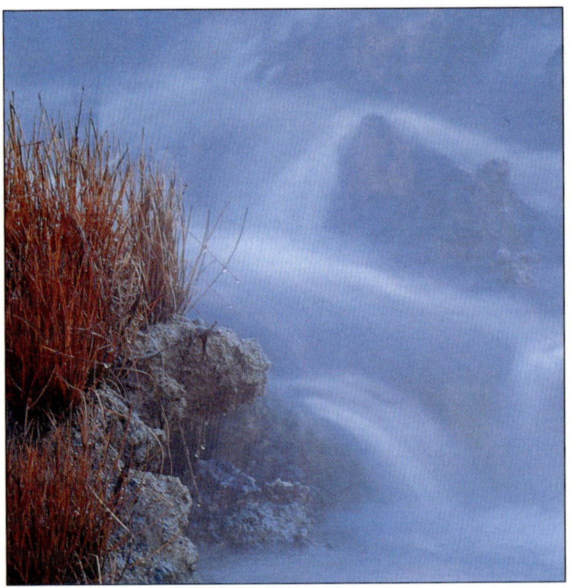

The stress of it all! You're overwhelmed with the scene's potential and your brain says "Ready - Fire - Aim!" I console myself that I need to get the first several images out of my system before I can settle down, relax, and think. So I document first, create second. You can

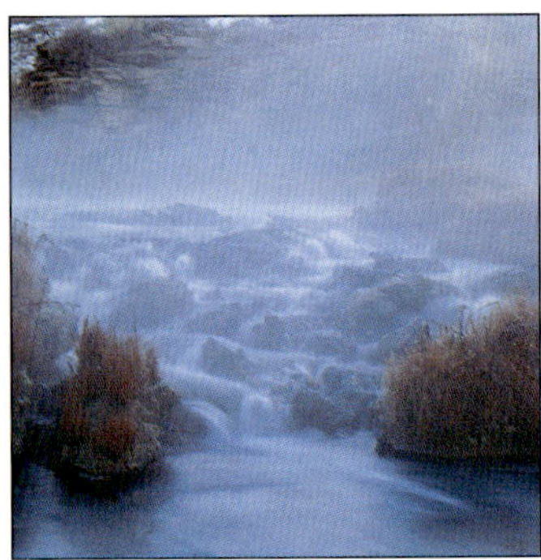

see what I started with in the small image. Fifty minutes and several lenses, different angles, and shutter speeds later, the top image was made at an exposure of EV10, 2 seconds @ f/45. The question I always ask myself: "What one or two elements best express the scene to me?"

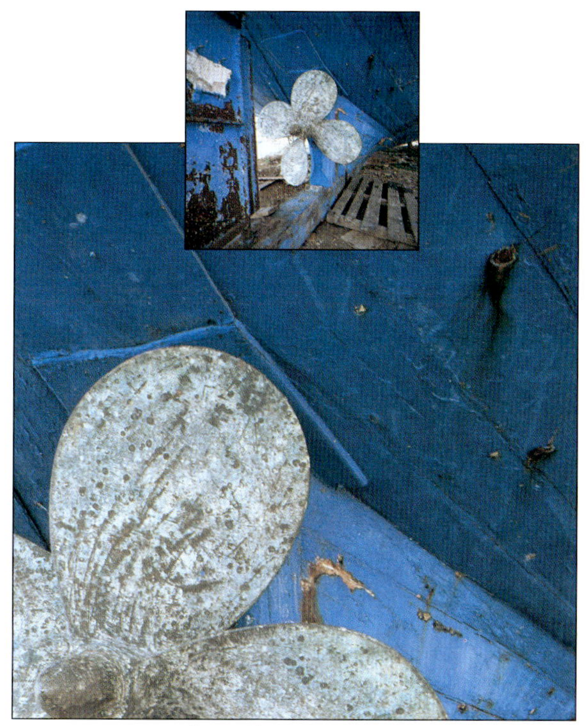

▼ Crop #1   ▲ Crop #2

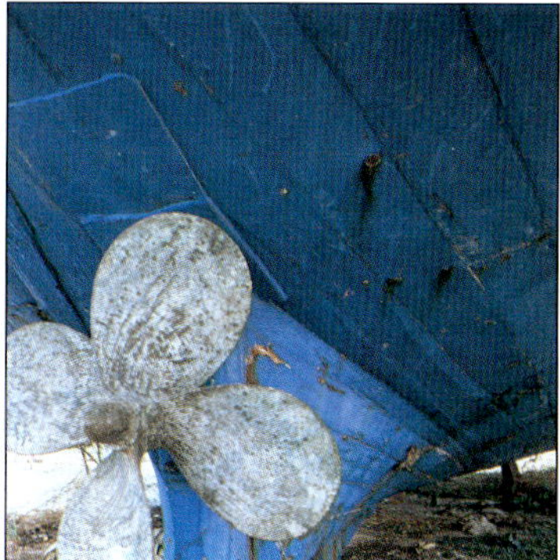

Different photographers, different styles. A good friend made the top image with the Superwide. He loves the converging lines toward the propeller. What attracted *me* was the prop's shape against the blue underside.

So right away I eliminated much of the background, then I cropped all of it. And you? How does your mind's eye visualize this scene? Crop twice and reveal a glimpse of your own individual style.

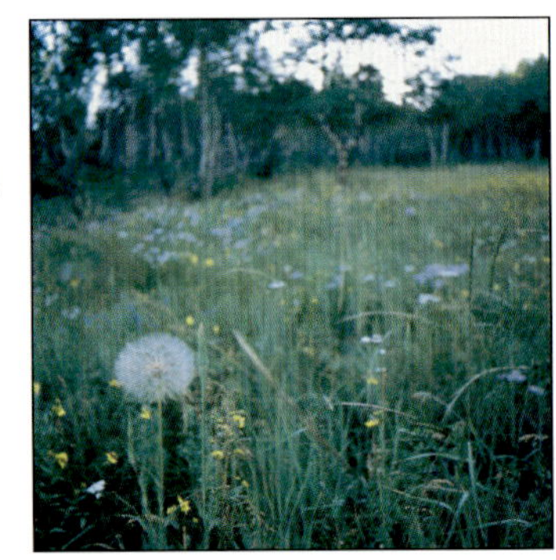

I think this scene has potential.

It's the globe shape

of the dying flower

I'm attracted to.

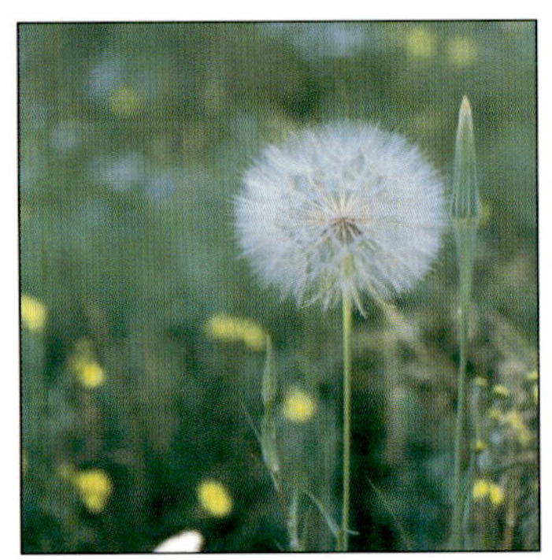

The 120mm lens with 1.0 Proxar

brings it in, but I see

hot spots in the lower third.

I'll add extension tube 16.

Much better.

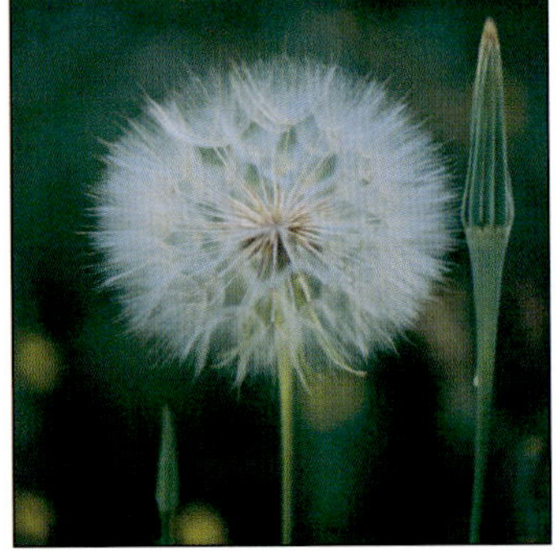

But the light's uninteresting.

Good timing to try

something a little different.

A break in the clouds?

Perfect.

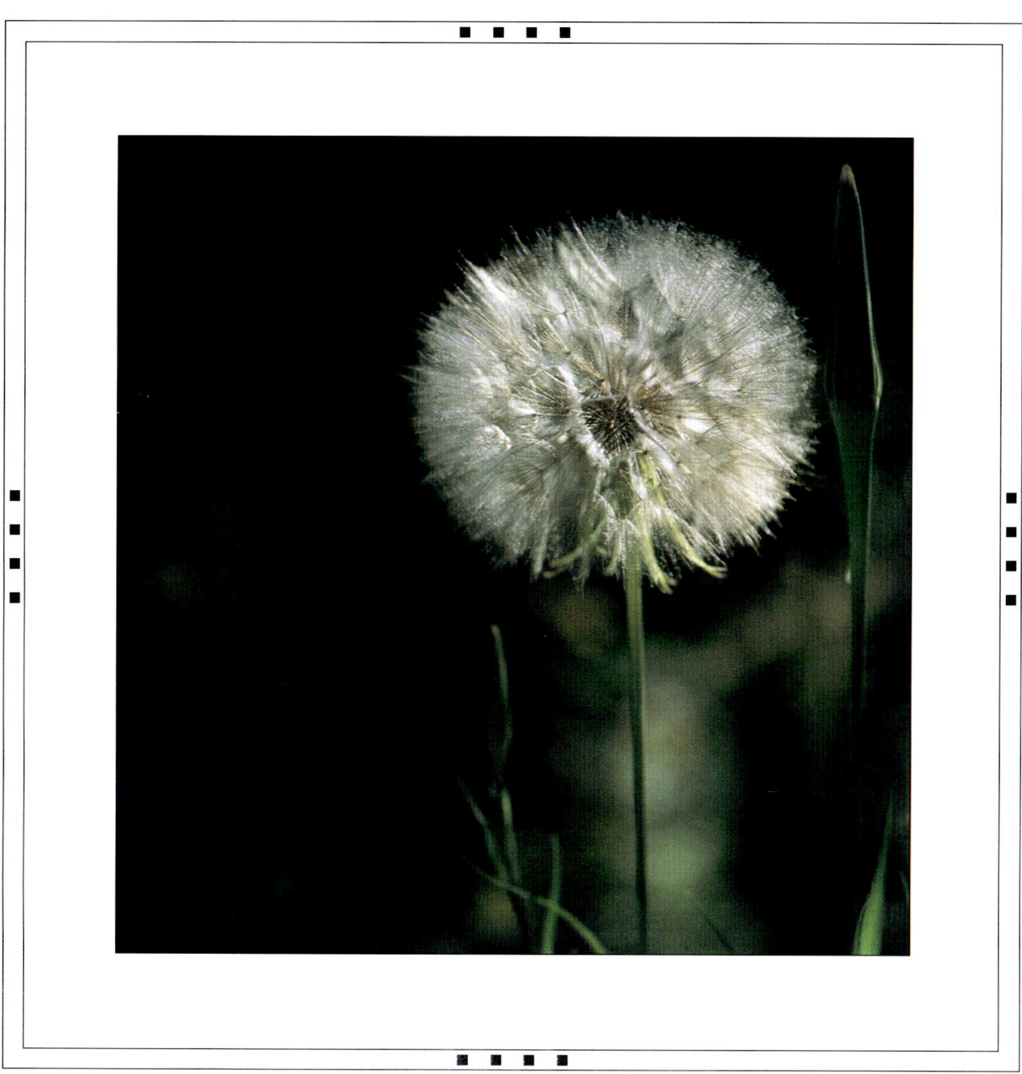

A Not-So-Subtle-Nuance

The correct exposure was 1/125 at f/8 or any combination letting in 13 EVs of light with ISO 100 film. But look what happened when I didn't pay attention to the background: I let the beargrass fall into a nondescript area and used an aperture that gave more depth

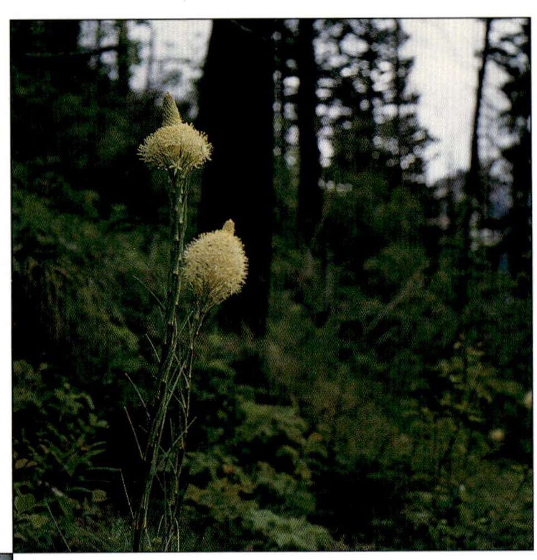

of field than an effective image would permit. A few extra minutes asking myself if this composition made a strong, clear statement yielded an aperture of f/4.0 to rid the scene of distractions, then I set the shutter to 1/500. Finally, I placed the subject in front of the dark trunk to emphasize it.

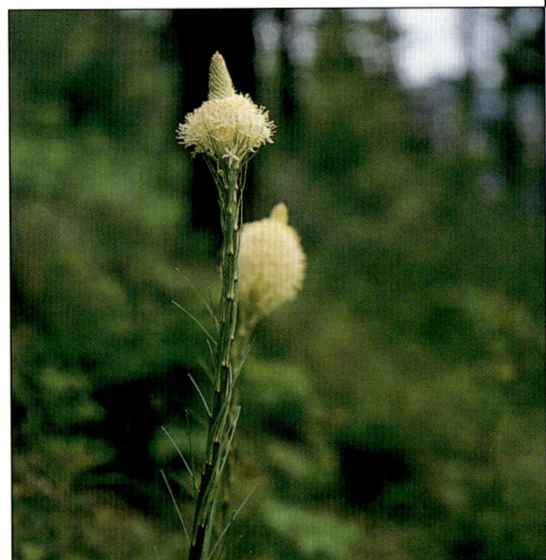

Smitten with the Shades

I liked these colors so well as I looked at the forest floor in Alaska's Katmai National Park, that I wasn't paying attention to the composition. After making this image at right, I paused and critiqued the scene in the viewfinder: the leaf points across the center – and I see some small distractions lower and upper – bland.

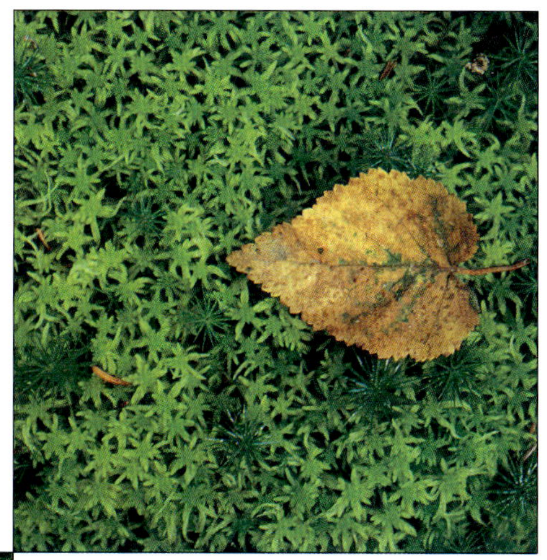

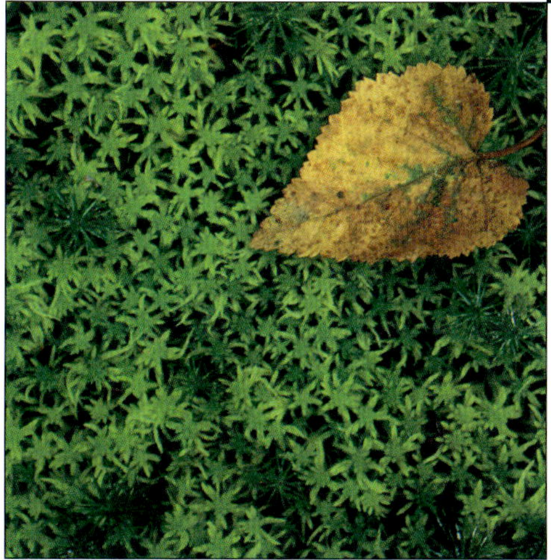

But I had most of the work behind me: my lens choice (120mm), magnification (Proxar 1.0), and rack and pinion focusing rail are all in place. So I pulled the pine needle out of the lower left, and aimed the leaf at an angle, which also covered the twig I couldn't remove. The image at left became 46-inch murals in two Maine airports.

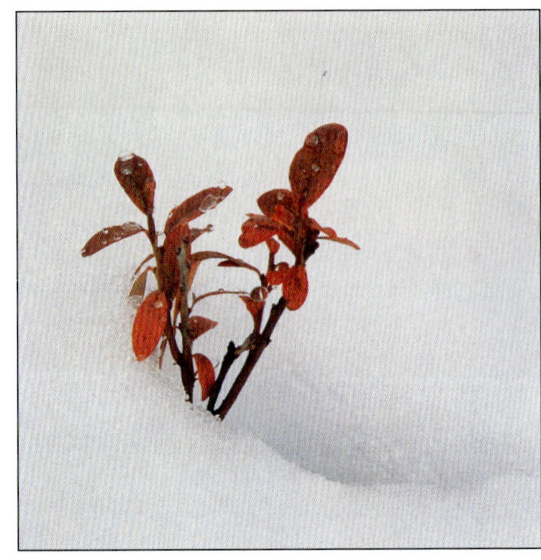

Once you know how to meter the scene 'correctly,' push those exposure police off your back and expose for mood. If your surroundings say 'bright, ethereal, oriental,' overexpose. Late August in Denali National Park, the fall season turned wintry overnight, as the tundra foliage poked above four inches of snow. The top picture shows an accurate depiction of the two colors. But I needed *sunglasses* that day of no sunshine. So I began with a half stop of overexposure and kept going. Which is 'right'? The lightest one expresses the day's mood best to me.

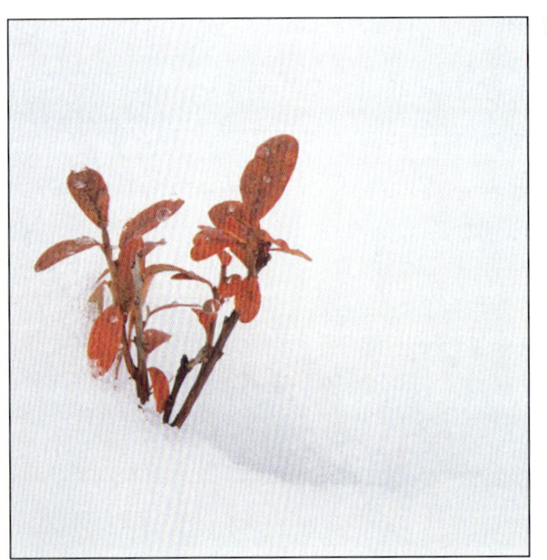

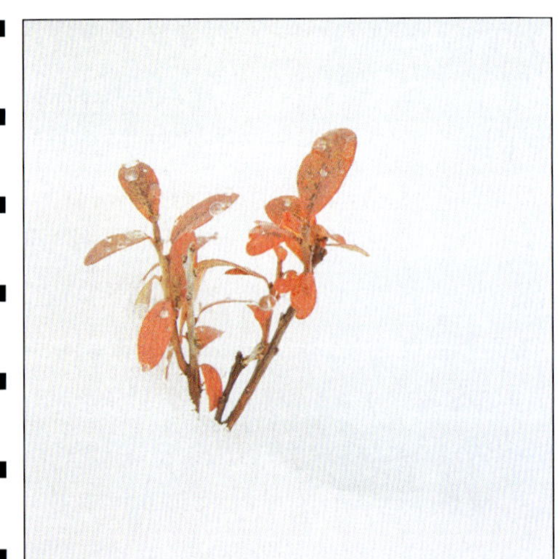

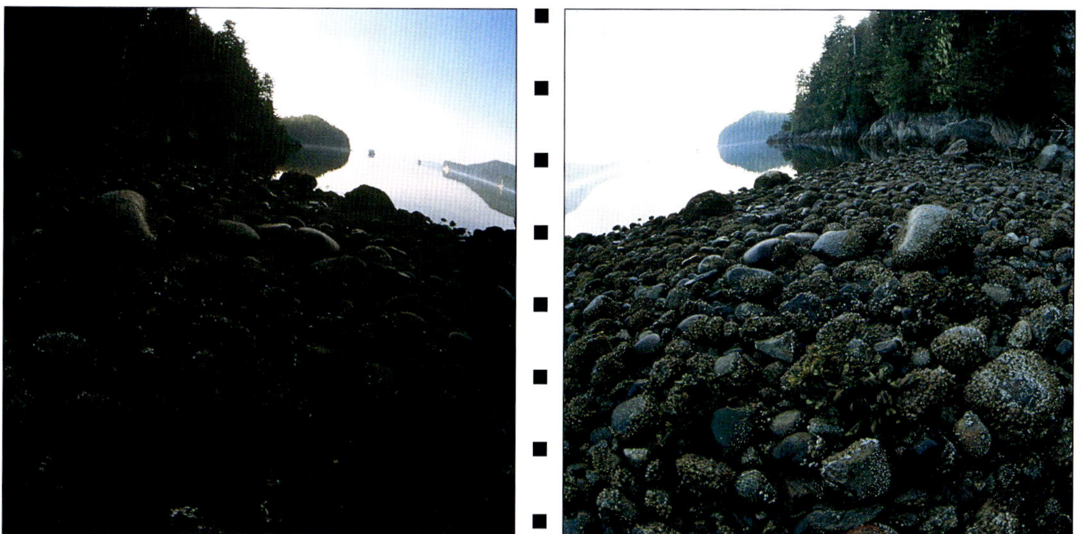

How often have we heard to expose for shadow detail on print film, for highlights on transparencies? Why not expose for all or none? If personal expression is your objective, why not treat exposure as a part of composition – and play? Some of my friends describe themselves as 'five degrees off center' – maybe your images are most expressive at 'a stop off the EV.' Once you know how to meter to achieve an effect, then tinker. ■ Two good friends said the most significant change in how their images pleased them came from experimenting with light hitting the film. First, they learned *how* to make clean exposures, then they were free to move on and develop their style. In their own words: "We now know how to achieve the effect we want. Before, it was luck and bracketing."

The Shine That Blinds Lackluster scenics, wet leaves, and glare on objects, including water – all can be improved with the discriminating use of a polarizer. Leave one on all the time and it reminds me of people who swear too much: it loses its punch. Because the sun is close to a ninety-degree angle from the buoys and from my view of the sky and the clouds, this scene is an excellent polarizer candidate.

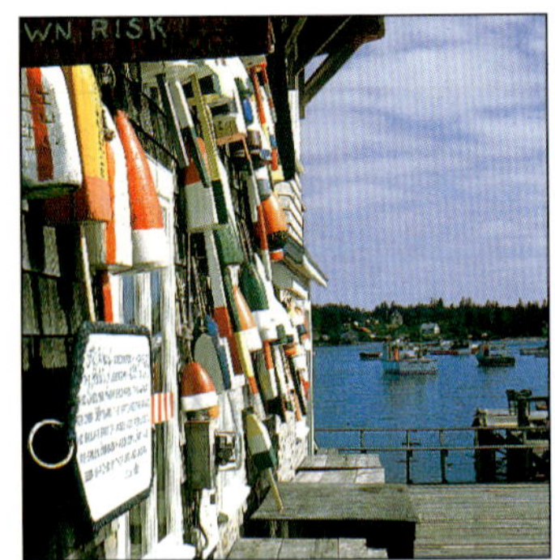

What Happened? This wasn't the Matterhorn the way I saw it at all. Where did that golden nugget go? The meter read the town's darker areas and wanted me to give enough exposure to bring out detail in the buildings. It makes sense that if the meter reads darker than 18% reflectance, it asks for a longer exposure. Unfortunately, the meter didn't know my subject was only the peak.

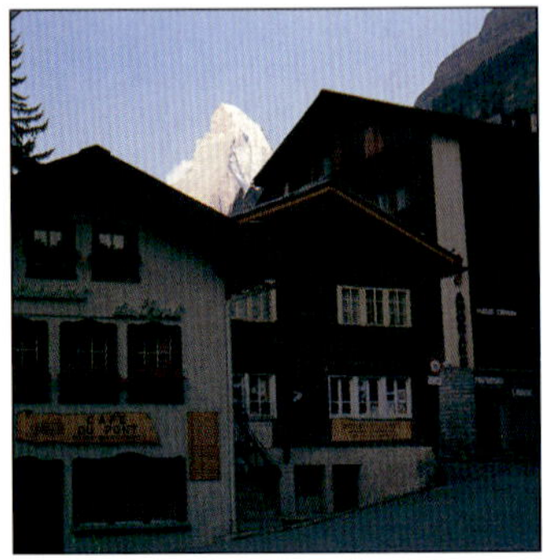

Bright sun, side lit – open up a stop and it's easy, right? It works fine when the subject fills the frame, but not when the 'subject' is both the fore and the background. If I open up to expose Julie's *face* correctly, which is side lit, I'll overexpose the rest of the scene.

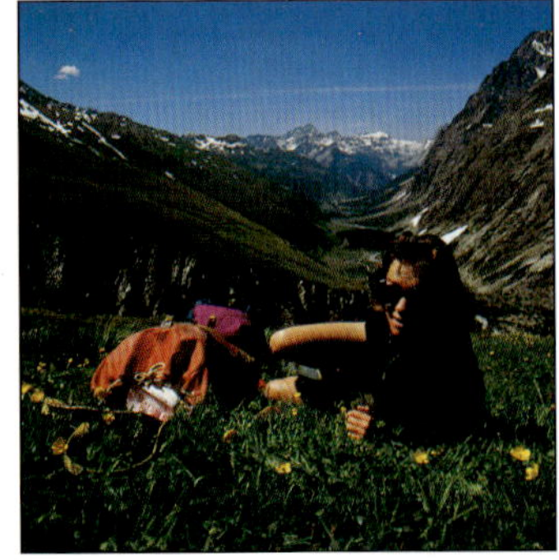

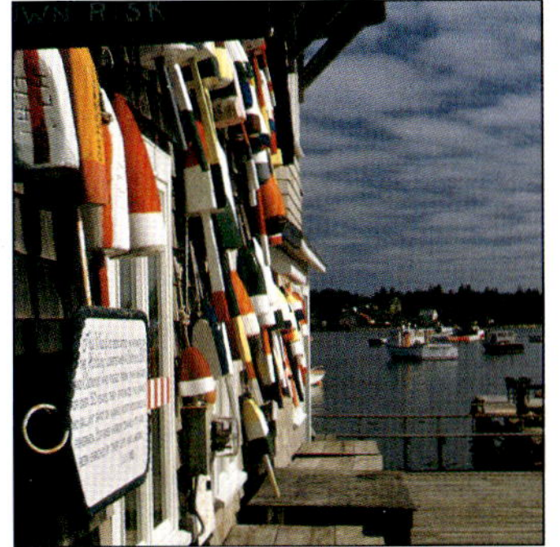

Wow! The glare's gone. I'm losing 1.5 stops of light by polarizing, but on a tripod, my slower shutter speed doesn't matter. By the way, I lose the full stop and a half just by adding the filter, whether I turn the polarizer to achieve a slight or great effect. A polarizer is also useful for enhancing detail in distant scenics and sometimes helpful for rainbows – but too much and the rainbow's gone!

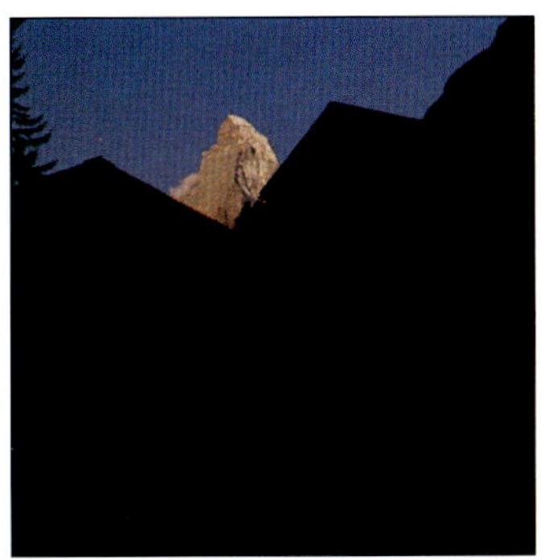

Aha! I have pointed the in-camera meter at the sky, without any foreground in it – I could have also used a spot meter and zeroed in on the peak. Immediately, the clutter in the foreground is reduced to black, which produces a bold, clean image with my 120mm lens. For more of a statement about the mountain without the town, use a 500mm lens as I did on page 45. If you want *both* areas acceptably exposed, add a graduated neutral density filter to 'calm down' the sky and the peak. See page 7.

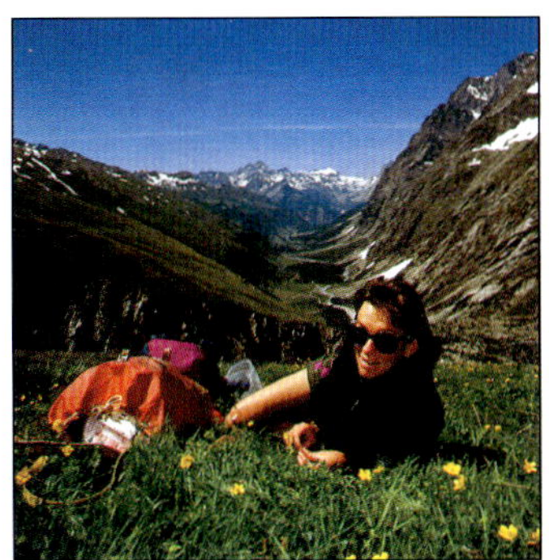

The correct exposure for half of Julie and all the background is Basic Daylight Exposure: 1/125 at f/16 (see back cover). But the side of Julie's face needs a hit of light to eliminate the shadow. So I set the flash at two stops more open than the aperture setting – f/8 for this example. A 1:4 ratio or –2 on the flash dial does the same thing.

Toss it! When a beautiful scenic comes back as bland, often it's due to too much sky or foreground. The subject would 'pop' on its own, but it doesn't fill the frame. A third – a third – a third just doesn't cut it. Here I need to eliminate the duck swimming in the foreground and the excess sky above the mountains.

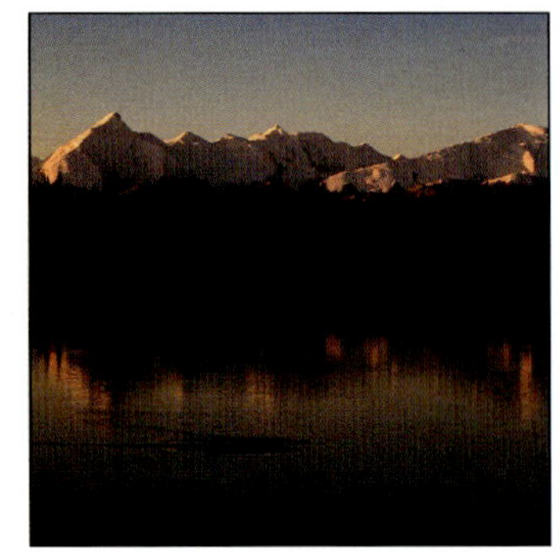

Details, Holmes! Carelessness and excitement can lead to an inappropriate depth of field. My interest in this scene is the ice formed on the hanging snow, but I metered and mindlessly dialed in the EV of 10 on my 120mm lens barrel. I didn't notice what I chose was the combination of one second at f/32. But look how this extreme depth of field affected the composition. The result: way too much background definition competing with my subject.

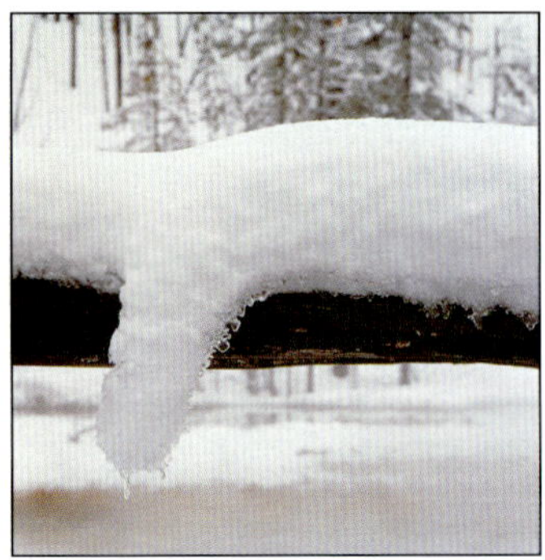

Zzzzz... Here's a dull, empty view looking up the Rhône Valley into Martigny, Switzerland, on a hike around Mont Blanc. Spectacular scenery, but no focal point, no message about the trip or my companions, and no redeeming soft light. If I had moved in on the alpenrose to fill the foreground, I may have salvaged the image. But in midday sun, with nothing to hold your interest, this dies.

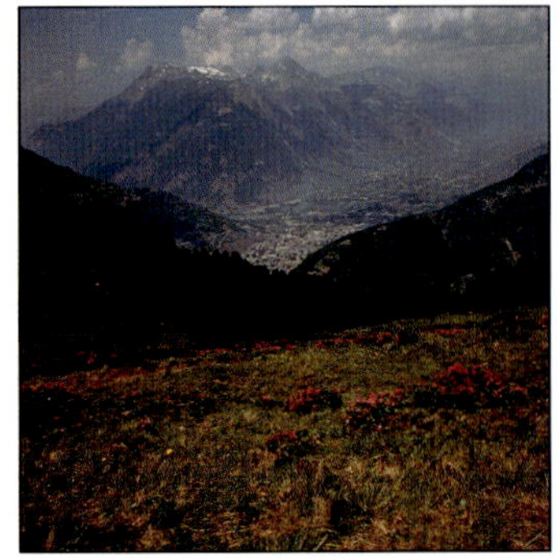

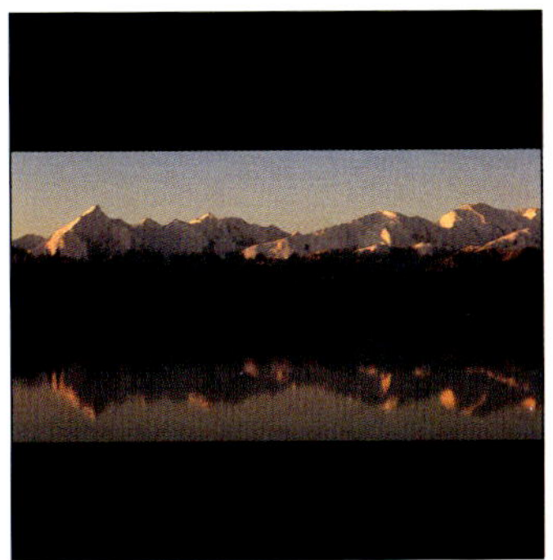

Mask it! Why buy a separate pano camera when a mask will do? I've fallen in love with this little accessory and I use it for both horizontals and verticals. Granted, the viewfinder mask only fits for the horizontal, but it doesn't take a mathematician to figure out the middle half of the frame will be the image, no matter on which axis you're working.

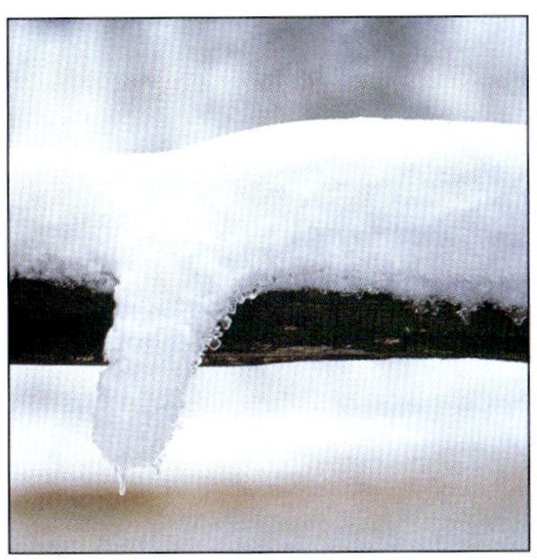

Voilà! Same exact Exposure *Value*, but the combination here is 1/60th of a second at f/4. Using the depth of field preview button, I locked in the EV of 10 and turned the lens barrel until the background became indistinct. I think of the shutter speed as the 'man in motion' – stopping action or blurring it – and the aperture as the 'man as artist' component, the artistic half. When in sync with the subject, the image works.

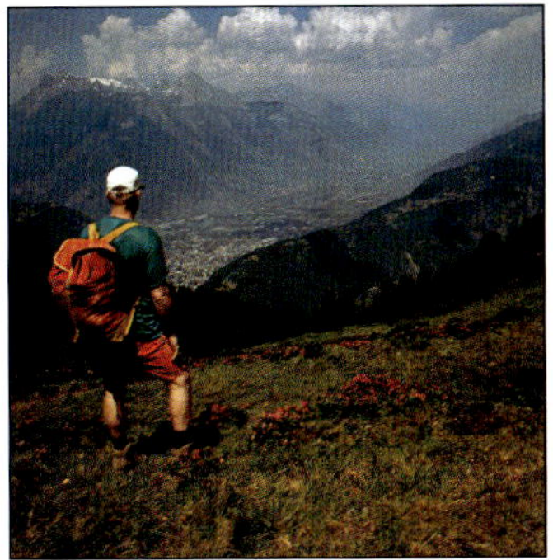

Thanks, Tom, for bailing me out. He spoke volumes about our weather, the trip's duration (five days of smelly clothes in that old backpack), and the view's expanse. I asked Tom to face the same direction I did, in order to highlight the scene the way I saw it, to show off his hiking gear, and to lead your eye into the frame.

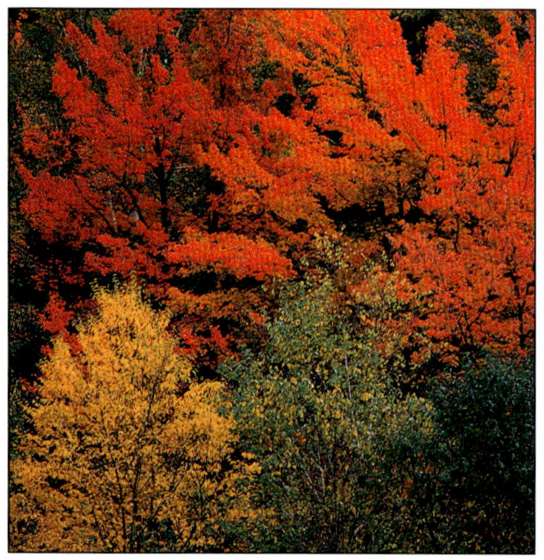

When you're in a new location with no idea where to begin, or you haven't much time to organize your thoughts, or you're on vacation with non-photographers – think up a theme and make some photographs. It's a little like walking into a hardware store having sketched out a list: you have a starting point. These three images give an idea of how I tackled similar situations, making up themes of Winter Patterns, Autumn Colors, and Just Pastels. I worked through mental blocks in new places to come home with images I like.

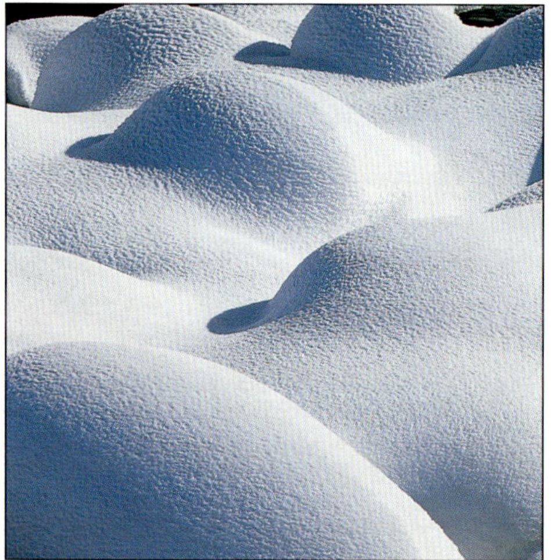

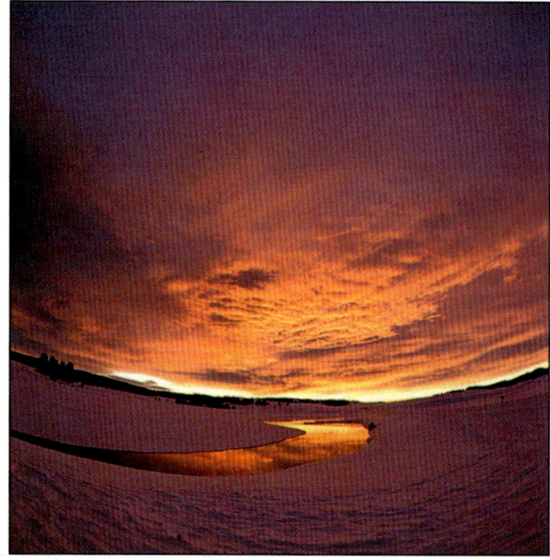

Stuck in a rut? Ask three friends what they like most about your work. Is it how you capture mood? Balance colors? Simplify a scene? What they see in your work helps define your style. Study the art, clothing, architecture, and writing you like. Adapt the common threads to your photography. I like simple, vigorous writing, sleek clean lines in cars and architecture, and unadorned, uncluttered clothing. This is reflected in my photos. Move consciously toward expressing the character *you* are in the images you create.

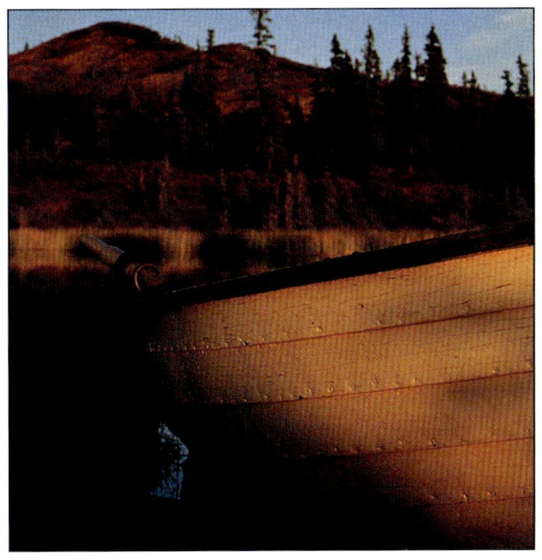

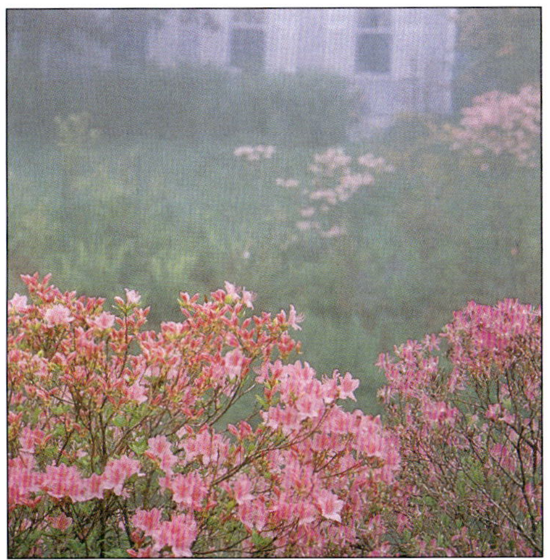

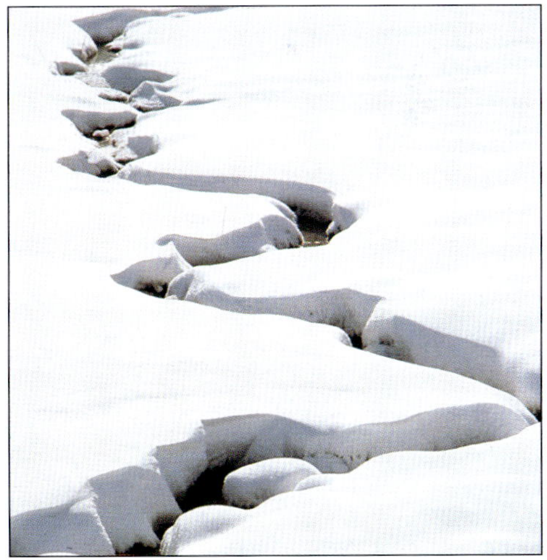

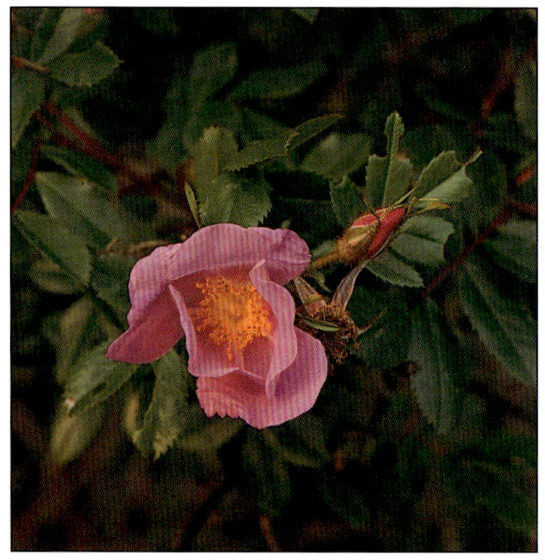

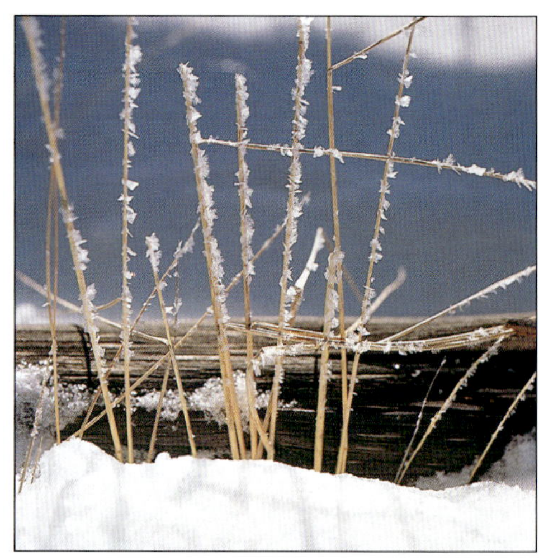

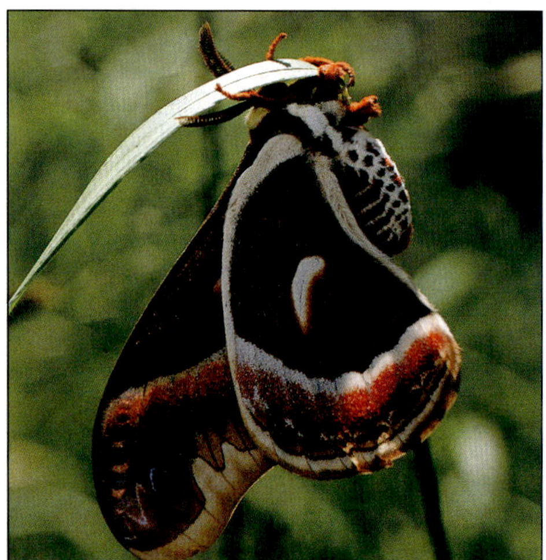

Many people think they haven't the patience for close-ups: too technical and time consuming to get good results. I maximize my chances of making a satisfying image by surveying the scene carefully without the camera first. Do I want the whole moth or just a small pattern in it? If there is a breeze, can I shelter the subject with myself or a light disk? I usually move in toward life size gradually - composing a petal's dewdrop can be more challenging than composing the entire rosebud. First, I'll add a Proxar filter (page 44), using either a mirror or a light disk to warm the underside or to shade the hot spots. Even light allows nature's hues to

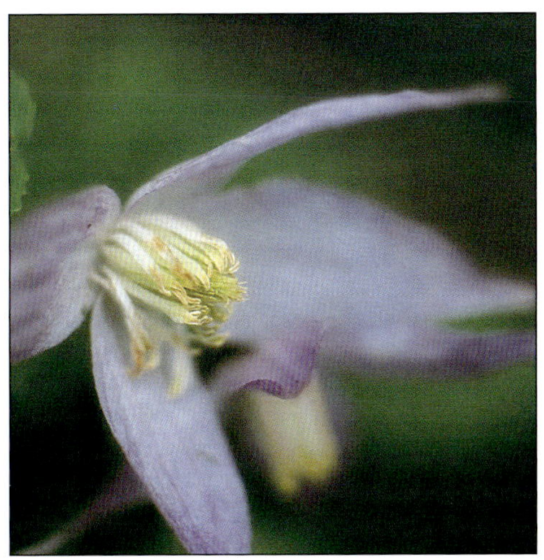

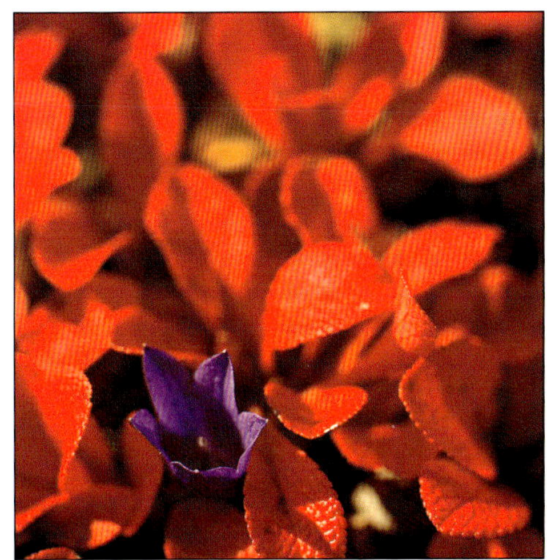

'blossom.' A focusing rail (page 45) will allow moving the camera small increments instead of repositioning the tripod. Extension tubes on longer lenses permit greater working distance from the subject. Tubes can be stacked for greater magnification. Maximize depth of field by keeping the lens parallel to the subject. Take advantage of shallow depth to highlight just one part of the scene. Look for leading lines, a pattern, or try experimenting with a Softar filter. Exposure is aided with a gray card (pages 7 & 13). Permit yourself to be unsettled with the initial results. You didn't master fly fishing or cross country skiing in one outing, either.

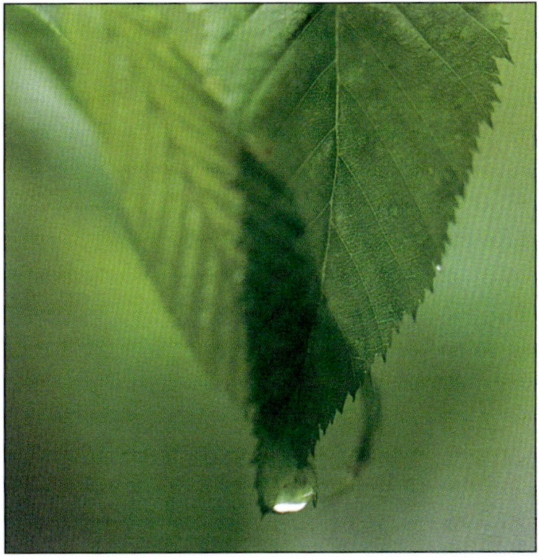

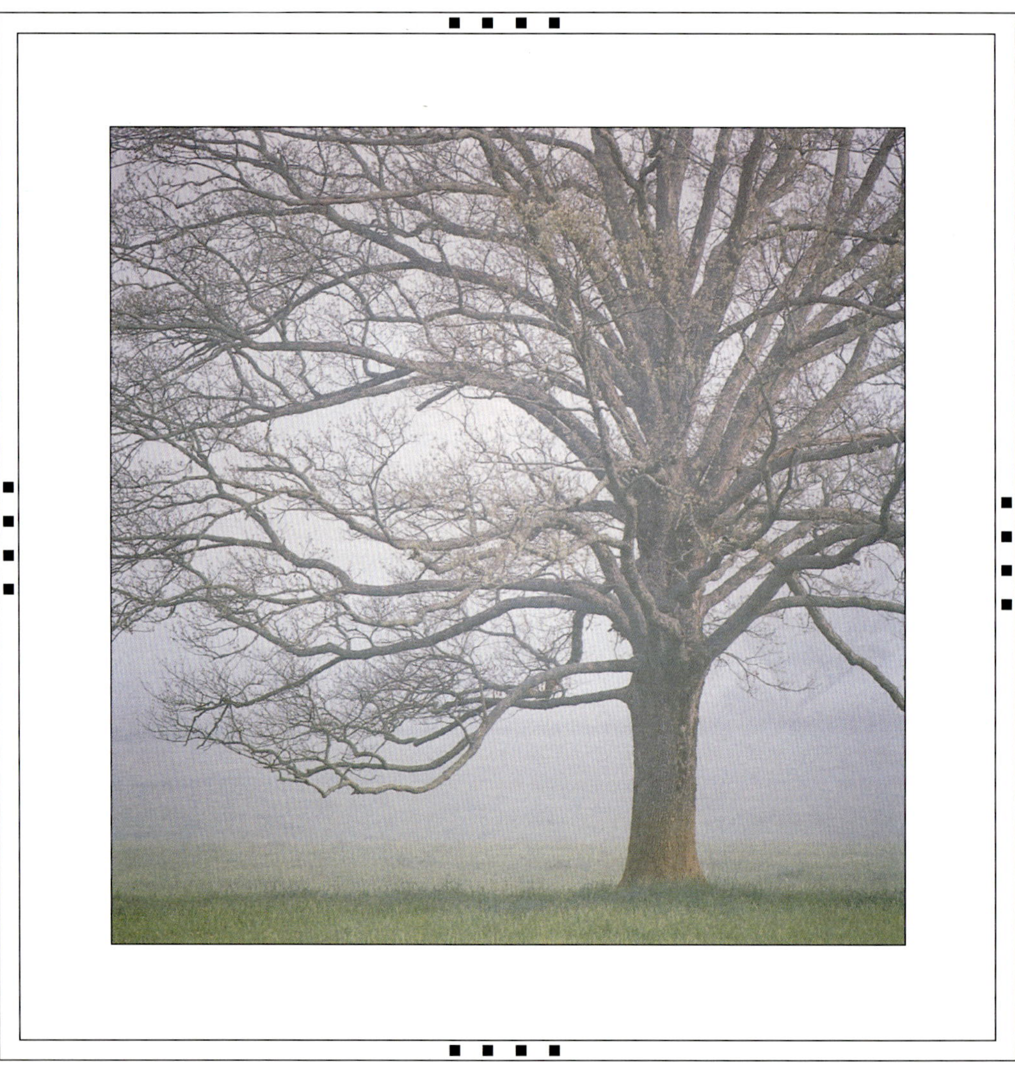

E veryone asks it: what do you buy – slide or print film? Where do you get it processed? How do you catalog and file the results? Let's start here: there seems to be a mystique about the more 'advanced' you are, the more you 'should' prefer transparency film, and that if you photograph a lot, slide film is less expensive. ■ My take: the final product should determine the film choice. I use more slide than print film because I publish and project, but the cost of buying and processing a roll of 120 slides is almost identical to buying a roll of negative film, and paying for developing with five inch proofs from a wedding/portrait lab. ■ If my products were prints for my wall, for gifts, for albums, or for showing to my friends, I'd buy mostly print film. The greater exposure latitude, ability to retouch the final image, and quality and ease of enlarging directly from a negative are additional advantages. ■ The key is to choose a professional lab – for E-6 slide processing, it will be a Kodak Q-Lab process monitoring system facility. For prints, look for a Kodak Promise of Excellence member lab. No need to fear your arctic fox and black bear will print poorly, either – their coloring shares a lot in common with brides and grooms. On the next pages are suggestions for filing and presenting your work.

You're interested in this topic, but you groan at the thought of it – I know very few photographers who like filing either slides or prints, but this is the organizational grunt work that pays off. For no other reason, an effective system avoids the overwhelming frustration of knowing you have an image but can't put your finger on it. ■ For prints, I use labs which first indicate the roll and frame number on the back of the proof and then individually bag the negative with the same information. I use 'shoe boxes,' that I label with the location and date on top, which are available from archival supply firms. On the next page are ways to file mounted, unmounted, and duplicate transparencies. The keys are logic, simplicity, habit.

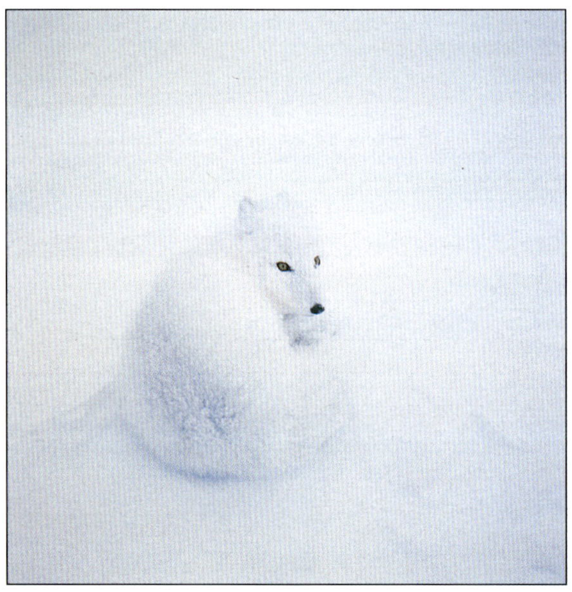

When you think of an image you made, is it by location (Tracy Arm, Alaska), the date (August of 1995), or the subject (Blue Sunset)? Answer this question and you're on your way to a simple filing solution. Here are some specifics to consider. For hardware, I use archival boxes for mounted slides by subject, and slide pages for unmounteds. Duplicate slides are filed in pages up front. ■ For labeling, you can put either computer-software generated or handwritten information on labels, on the slide mount, or on the slide page. I write directly on my glass-mounted slides to prevent a label from jamming in the projector. I keep a log book to record new entries, where they are (filed or sent out), and the date. ■ For categories, I find it's easier to list subject first, location second, date third: "Blue Sunset#1, Tracy Arm AK 895."

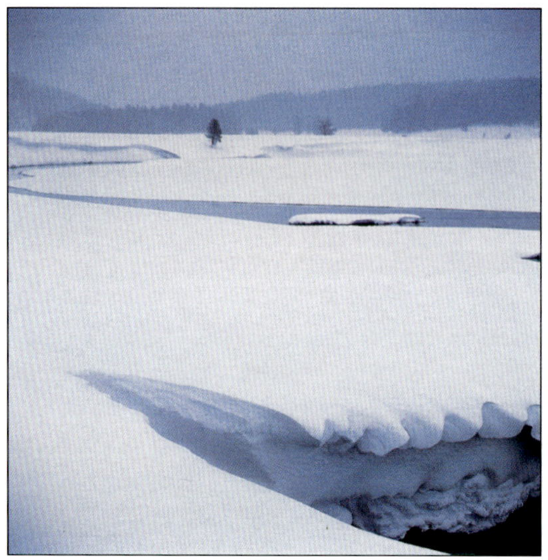

You never know when your years of amateur status may abruptly end! Be prepared with a tasteful, current portfolio of your best work. "Best" is what pleases you and suits the audience. ■ Show only your favorites – or I guarantee you'll be disappointed with what's chosen! I present 70mm medium format duplicate slides, slotting them into black mats with one to twelve openings. My maximum presentation to date has been five 12-opening pages, grouped by subject (animals, scenics, close-ups). For a more finished look, I sandwich the transparencies between two Light Impressions™ mats and slip them into a polypropylene sleeve. ■ I use a black folio folder which holds five double mats when I present in person. Through the mail, I send the mats in between two layers of cardboard with packing filler, in a medium-sized overnight shipping box. No need to overpack, just protect. My cover letter details the contents and when/how I'd like them returned.

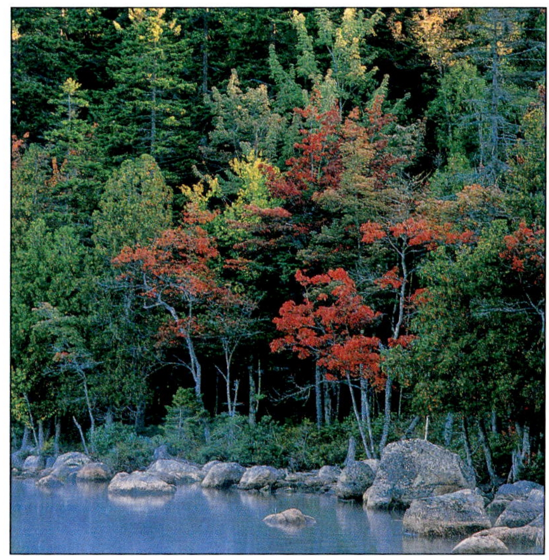

For a general print portfolio, start with a five inch print and use a mask or make crop marks to eliminate distractions, hot spots, or problems. Ask the lab what paper surface would enhance the image. Three choices are glossy (F), smooth semigloss (N) and lightly textured (E). Then use that combination consistently in one portfolio. ■ If you are working from a transparency, an internegative will allow a print lab to make your enlargement. An eight inch print looks handsome centered left, top, and right on an 11x14 inch white photographic paper background. There's room below it to sign, label, or date. ■ If a print competition is your goal, send the rules to your lab and discuss the options. Full-service labs can mount your images on board, foam core, canvas or gatorfoam for greater durability. Ask for samples. ■ Portfolio boxes are available in a variety of sizes to accommodate up to ten matted prints. Light Impressions™ makes a Thinline Portfolio Box which can go in a special carry bag when travelling. To ship, I use the same method as described on the previous page.

■ *501*c ■

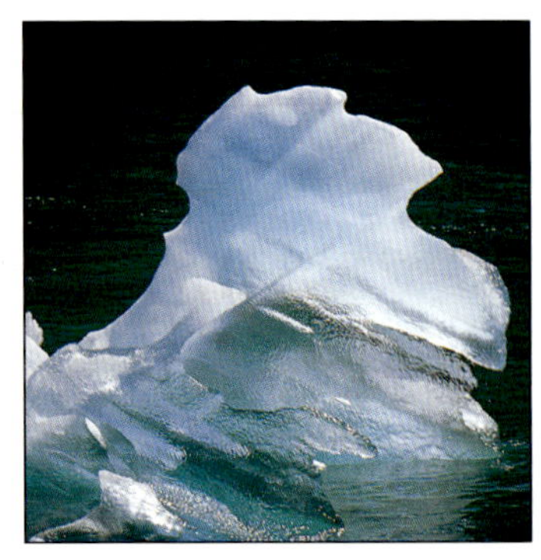

Stepping up to medium format? Here's the ideal way into the 'system'. The Hasselblad 501c camera body is packaged with 80mm lens and 12-exposure film magazine. It's a completely battery-free, mechanical single lens reflex camera with all the interchangeability of other Hasselblad models – from lenses and film magazines, to viewfinders and focusing screens. I use this as my primary camera. It's great in cold weather, the design is simple, and it's plenty compact to hike, ski, or bike with. Weighs 3 lbs. 4 oz. with 80mm lens and A12 film magazine.

■ *503*cxi ■

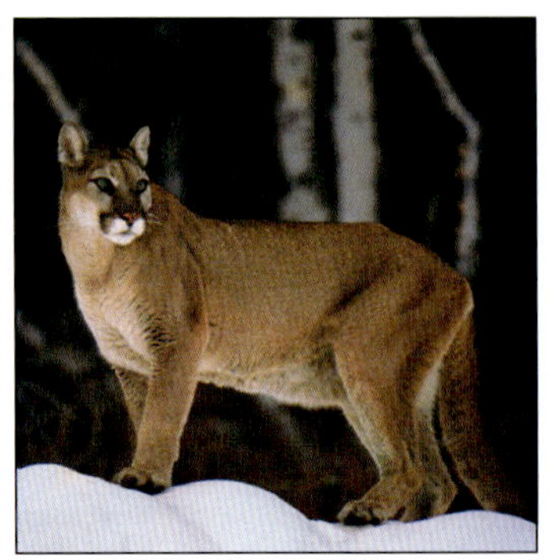

For a nature or wildlife photographer who needs dedicated flash capability, the 503cxi is the way to go. A sensor in the battery-free camera body controls the output of the flash unit so you can balance daylight with fill flash or make either one the dominant light source. It automatically compensates for light loss caused by filters, tubes and bellows. Love close focus work in poor light? The 503cxi will make you look like a pro. I use a Metz 40 MZ-2 flash with SCA390 adapter. Weighs 3 lbs. 5 oz. with 80mm lens and A12 film magazine.

■ *903*swc ■

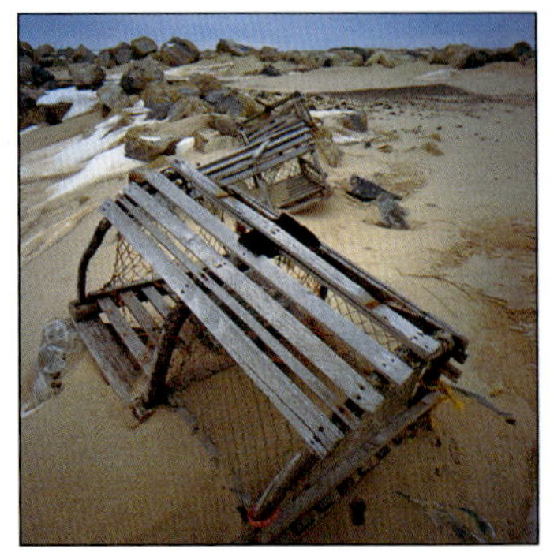

"Extremely compact, super high resolution,"– the Superwide is all this and more. The Biogon 38mm true wide angle lens is permanently attached – and considered the finest optic Zeiss makes for Hasselblad. The lens exhibits absolutely no distortion for people candids, backcountry scenics, and, with an underwater housing, the marine world. The enormous depth of field from 26 inches to infinity at f/22 allows catching fleeting moments without focusing. When time and energy are scarce but I just can't give up the format or quality, I count on the 903. Weighs 3 lbs. with A12 film magazine.

■ 50mm CF ■

Perfect for telling a story in one image, with foreground interest leading into a sweeping scenic. Terrific for groups of people, or just one person, to add perspective to a landscape. Strengths: plenty of depth of field when desired, short and compact, with floating lens element for excellent close focusing.

Specs: 75 degree diagonal angle of view, apertures from f/4 to f/32. 3.75 inches long and weighs 1 lb, 12 oz. Takes a 60mm filter. I use a lens shade with all focal lengths.

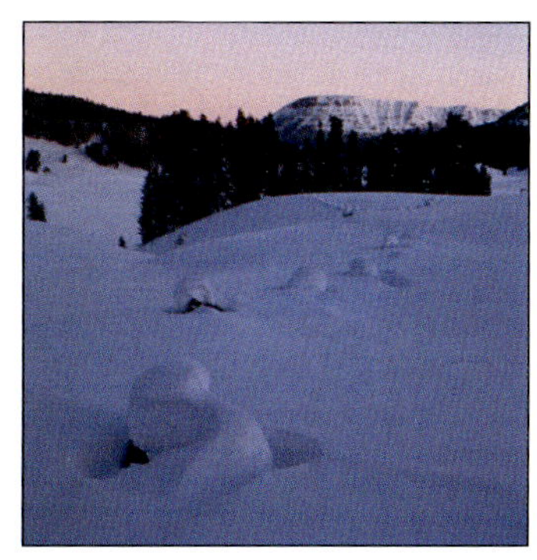

■ 120mm MAKRO PLANAR ■

This is the first lens I bought and it's still my favorite. Its strengths for flat-field closeups with no distortion are well known, but it's just as suited for candids and scenics. The teleconverter makes this a mid range telephoto very quickly. With extension tubes, there's still enough working distance from the subject not to disturb a dewdrop, a slug, or the dirt on a mushroom.

Specs: 37 degree diagonal angle of view, apertures from f/4 to f/32. 3.9 inches long and weighs 1 lb, 8.5 oz. Takes a 60mm filter.

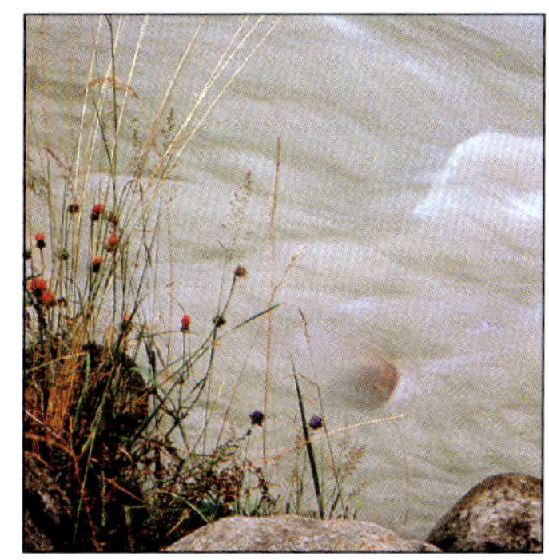

■ 500mm CF ■

A great wildlife and scenic lens. Many of my best images have been made with the 500. It's exceptional at both closing in on a distant mountain range and capturing polar bears on Hudson Bay. And with extension tubes, combined with internal focusing, the 500mm provides ample working distance from a closeup subject.

Specs: 9 degree diagonal angle of view, apertures from f/8 to f/64. 13 inches long and weighs 4 lbs. Takes a 93mm filter.

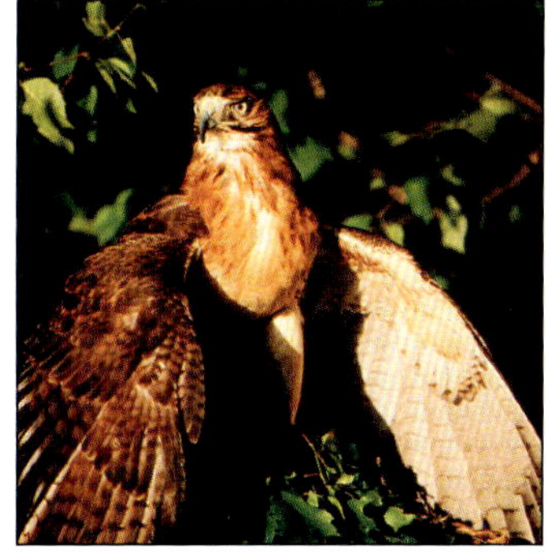

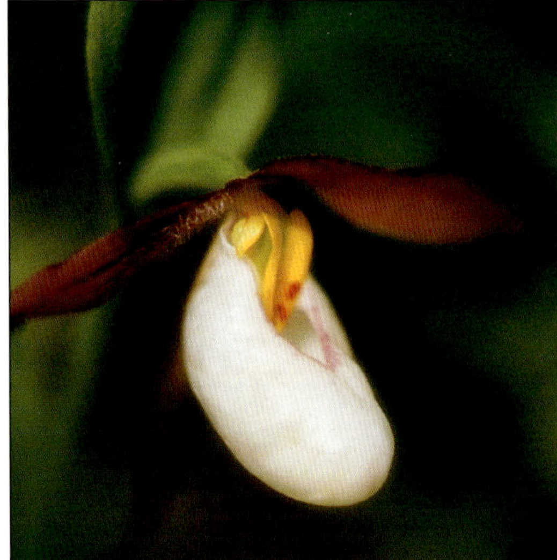

Film Magazines - I carry two A24s, one with print, one with slide film, and A12 with T-MAX or Pro 400 film. **Flash** - See page 42, middle section. **Tripod** - Gitzo carbon fiber with 1376 ball head and a quick release plate. **Filters** - *Proxar* - Closer focusing without light loss. With lens at infinity, subject is in focus at one meter with 1.0m Proxar. 0.5m and 2m are also available. I stack the 1.0 and 0.5 frequently. Lightweight, small, many uses. *Polarizer* - Reduces or eliminates reflections or glare. See page 28. *Softar* - for 'controlled image softening', people or closeups. When the mood is ethereal, it's fun. I, II, III available. I use #II. **Meters** - See pages 12-13 for a full discussion. *On the camera*, mine is a PME51 meter prism viewfinder center-weighted reflected meter indicating exposure by a row of EV numbers from 2-19, combined with a viewfinder giving an unreversed, 3x magnified focusing screen image. The unreversed image works well for photographing moving objects. *Hand held* - Gossen Luna-Star F2. **Other accessories** - *Spirit Level* - Attaches to the left accessory rail of the camera, to keep horizons, trees and boats straight. Indispensable. *Extension tubes* - 8, 16, 32, and 56mm long. Used alone or stacked, life size (1:1) is achieved when the extension equals lens focal length: 80mm extension on an 80mm lens, for example. A half to one stop light loss. *Panoramic mask* - Fits between the camera body and film back. Crops the image to a 1:2 ratio panorama. Includes a clear mask for the viewfinder. See page 30. *Lens shade* - Shields the lens from extraneous light, affords great protection from rain and snow.

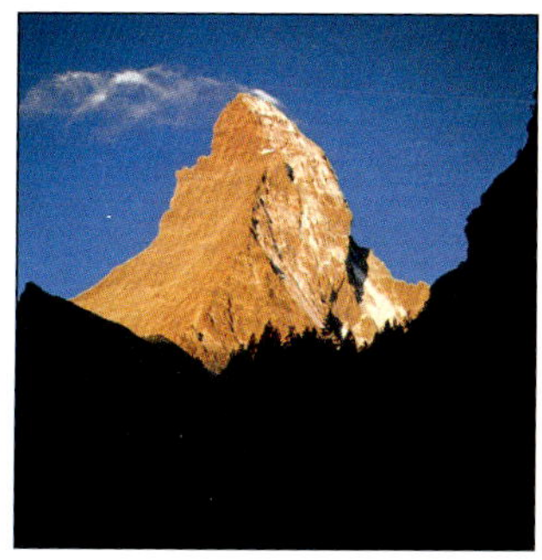

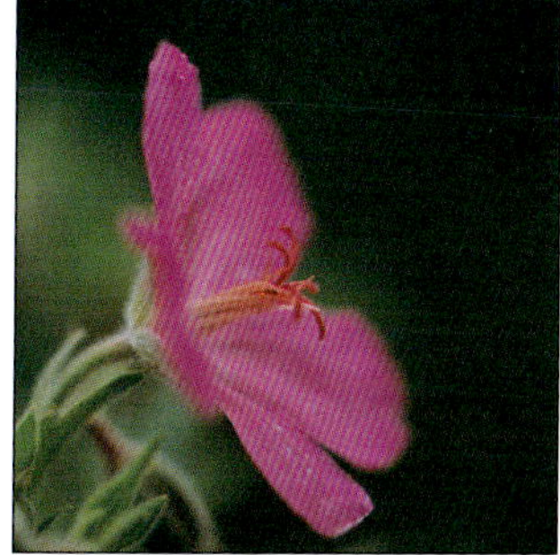

If macro photography, lifesize and greater, is your passion, invest in a bellows. It adjusts to between 63.5mm and 202mm. The bellows picks up where extension tubes leave off.

Why use a tripod? Because it slows you down to think about composition, allowing the use of shutter speeds to blur water (1 second+) and to capture fireworks (p.11).

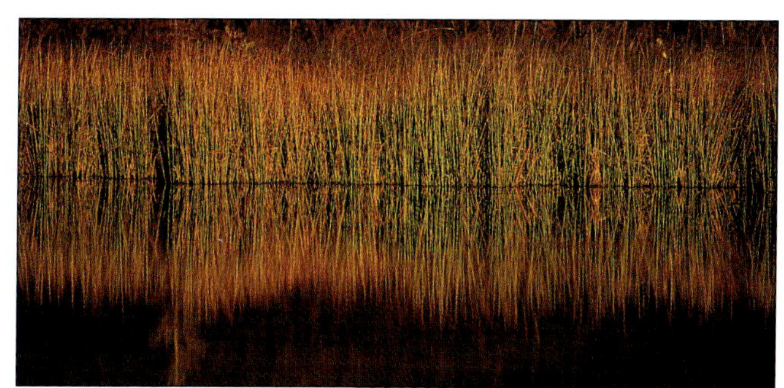

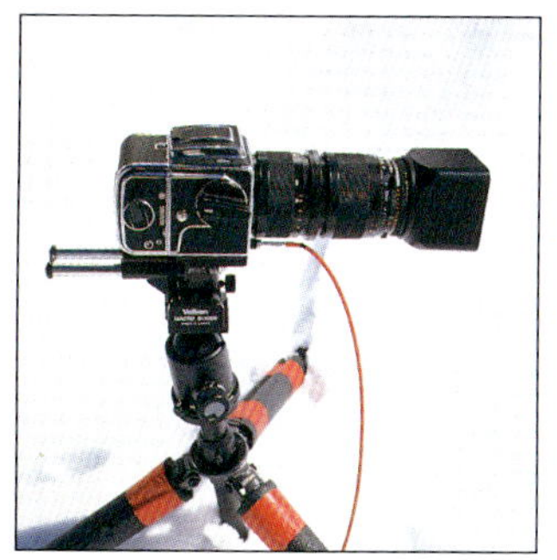

Frustrated with moving your tripod fractions of an inch to get maximum depth of field on a newt? Invest less than $100 in a rack and pinion focusing rail.

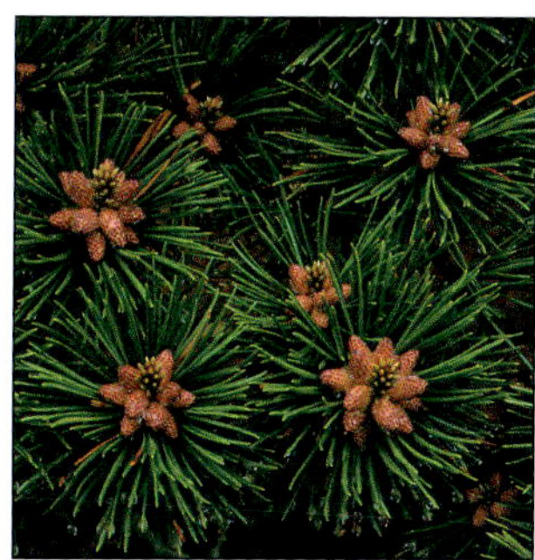

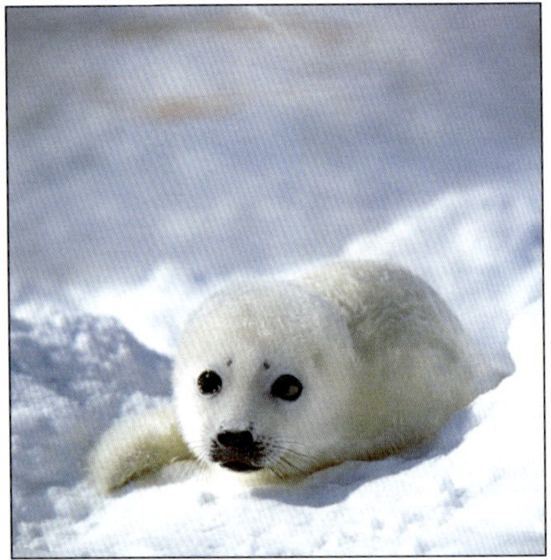

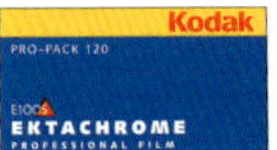

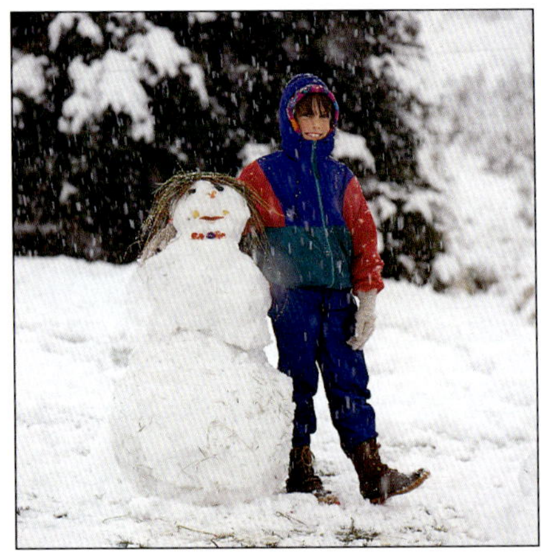

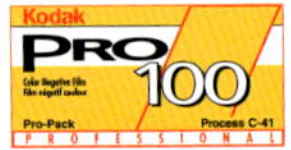

This brand new film will wow you – it's just plain *true*. While other transparency films exhibit a blue or lavender cast on the snow, Kodak Ektachrome professional E100S film produces a neutral, accurate white, and saturated blues, greens, and reds. Pushes very well. Available in 120, 35mm, and sheet formats. ■ The "T-grain" in all emulsion layers makes this film especially sharp. The "T" stands for tabular, which means the silver lays flat on the emulsion to produce a smoother, more refined surface. This is the color reversal film I choose for projection and publication.

I use Kodak Pro 100 film as my all-purpose outdoor color print choice. It offers excellent latitude, color saturation and contrast while using T-grain technology for its sharpness. It's balanced for daylight or electronic flash and I like it as well for natural skin tones as fine-art landscapes. ■ No need to push, as most C41 developers aren't set up for it anyway. Kodak's Pro 400 film, at two stops faster, is perfect for low light or moving subjects. I opt for print film when I want to make an enlargement or a scannable image, or to give a gift.

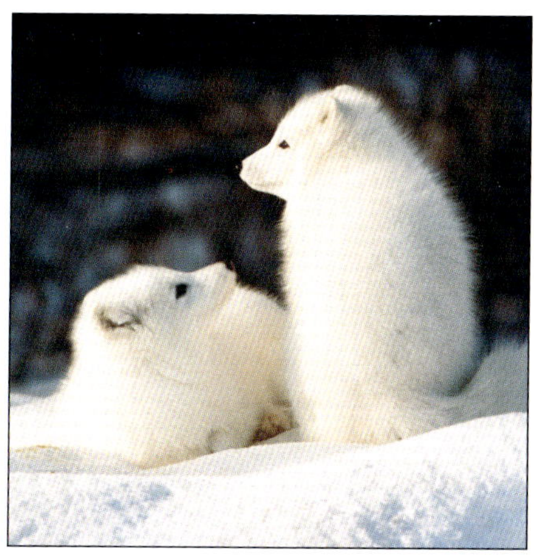

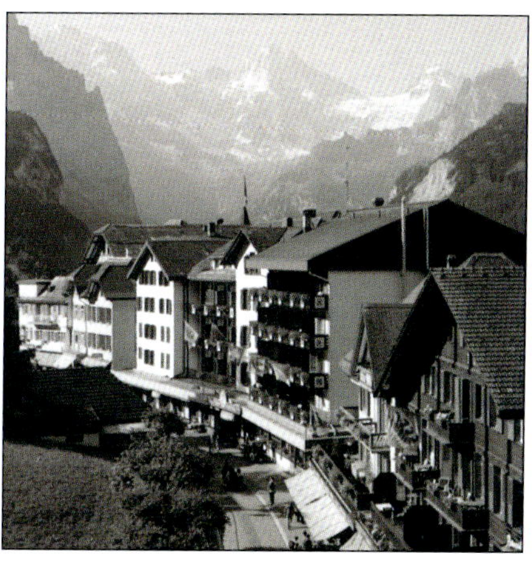

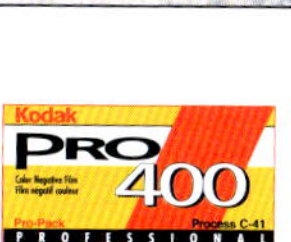

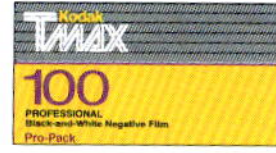

When I need my faster shutter speeds for photographing animals, I use Kodak Pro 400 film. My results show it's also well suited for sports and low-light subjects without a tripod. It too is balanced for daylight or electronic flash exposure, with fine grain and high sharpness attributed to its T-grain technology. ■ Early in the morning and late in the afternoon, I load a film magazine with PRO 400 film to use my longer focal length lenses without dropping below a 1/125th of a second shutter speed. Enlargements hold up very well.

We grew up with Kodak Plus-X and Tri-X pan professional films for black and white prints. Still excellent choices. But 100 speed Kodak T-MAX professional film goes further. With T-grain emulsion and very high resolving power, it permits a high degree of enlargement, with huge exposure latitude. ■ Coupled with Hasselblad's image quality, far-off details are 'resolved' with T-MAX film, which distinguishes between minute differences in the scene. It's the finest black and white film on the market. Need a faster ISO? Try 400 or p3200.

WARM WET	WARM DRY
COLD WET	COLD DRY

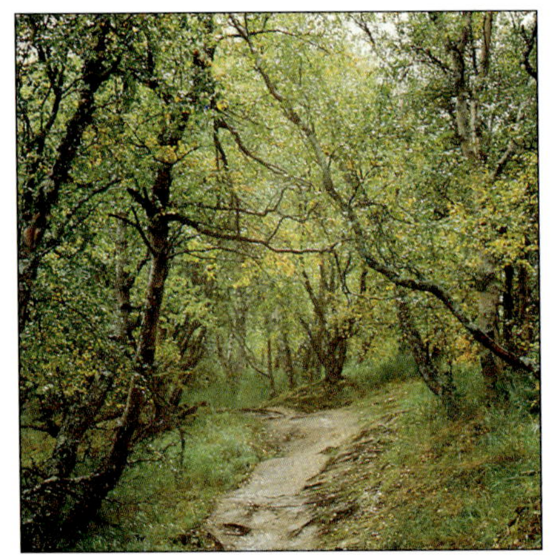

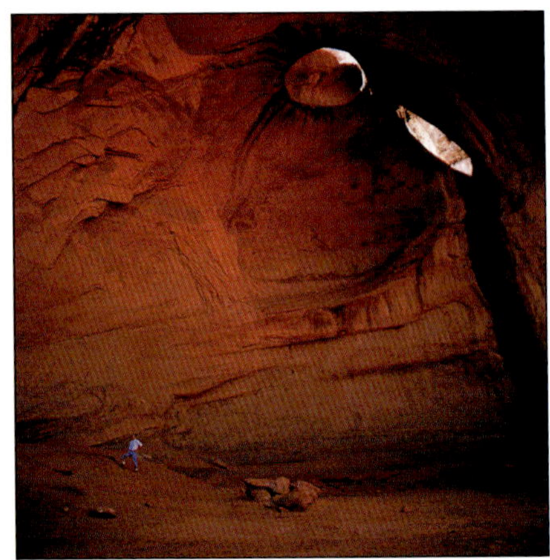

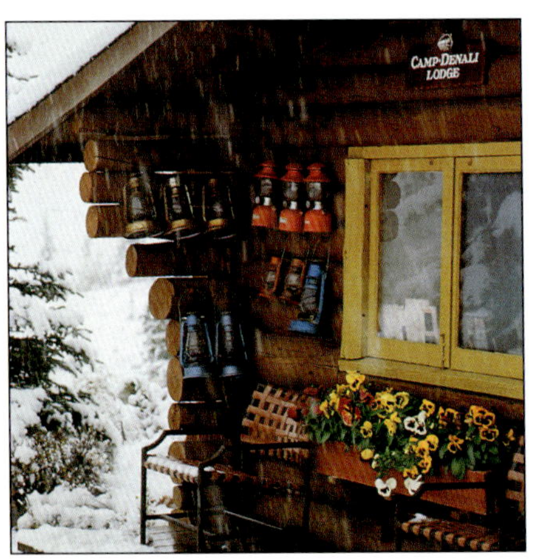

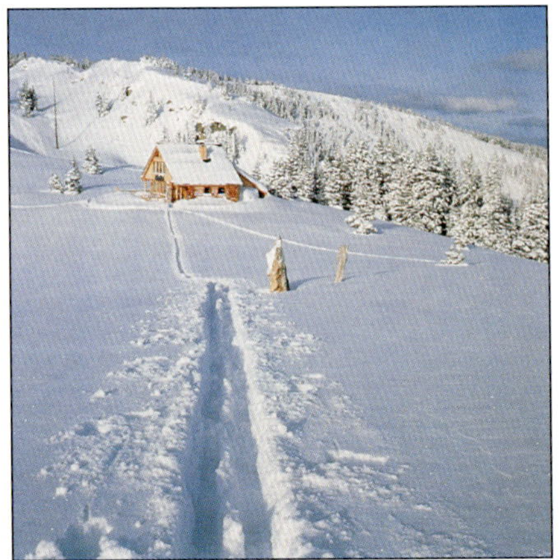

CLOTHING I WEAR

For comfort in any weather, start with the fabric next to your skin. This first layer keeps you safe by insulating your body against the cold and by wicking moisture away when you perspire. The top layer protects you from the elements, and the middle layers provide warmth. Regulate body temperature by immediately adding layers when you cool down and ventilating when you heat up - don't wait and don't be lazy.

■ ■ ■ ■ WARM WET

1. Polypro or fishnet briefs on bottom, CoolMax short sleeved shirt on top, CoolMax socks with ankle-high hiking boots or running shoes. 2. Lightweight cotton/stretch blend shorts or pants. 3. Packable Gore-Tex suit.

■ ■ ■ ■ WARM DRY

1. Polypro or fishnet briefs on bottom, CoolMax shirt with collar to protect against sunburn. CoolMax socks with ankle-high hiking boots or running shoes. 2. Lightweight cotton/stretch blend shorts or pants. 3. Visored hat.

■ ■ ■ ■ COLD WET

1. Polypro or fishnet briefs, expedition weight polypro top, same weight bottoms. 2. Primaloft top and bottoms, midweight fleece jacket on top. 3. Gore-Tex jacket with hood and pants. 4. Fleece hat, glove liners, fingerless hunting gloves, overmitts. Polypro liner socks, wool socks, cold weather boots.

■ ■ ■ ■ COLD DRY

1. Polypro or fishnet briefs, expedition weight polypro top, same weight bottoms. 2. Primaloft top and bottoms, mid to heavyweight fleece jacket. 3. Fleece hat, glove liners, fingerless hunting gloves, overmitts. Polypro liner socks, wool socks, cold weather boots.

Throughout the day, drink water to keep your energy up
or you'll wilt like a houseplant.

Here's how I prepare and what I take on a winter photography trip of a week to a month. I forget fewer items when I organize my packing from the top down. I keep asterisked * items with me in a carryon. Film is mailed to my destination a week ahead.

HEAD AND NECK

Fleece hat, visored cap	toothpaste and brush,
Goggles,* sunglasses,*	sunscreen for face and
contacts,* solutions*	lips, hairbrush, soap,
Toilet kit in a plastic bag:*	safety swabs, jackknife
face wash, dry skin	Fleece neck warmer
cream, shampoo,	Quart water bottle

TORSO

4 pr. briefs/undies	1 pr. jeans
1 fleece anorak	1 pr. flannel lined pants
Gore-Tex Stowaway suit	1 set Primaloft tops /
2 pr. med/expedition	bottoms
weight long underwear	T-shirt to sleep in
2 microfleece shirts	Snacks

HANDS AND FEET

2 pr. liner socks	2 pr. wool socks
1 pr. fingerless	1 pr. windproof overmitts
fleece gloves	1 pr. knee-length gaiters
1 pr. running/	1 pr. polypro glove liners
walking shoes	1 pr. cold weather boots

L.L. BEAN'S ROLLING DUFFEL

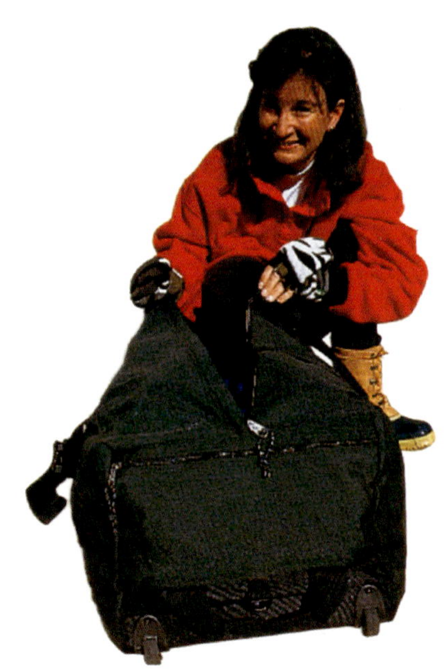

L.L. BEAN'S FRONT-LOADING BACKPACK

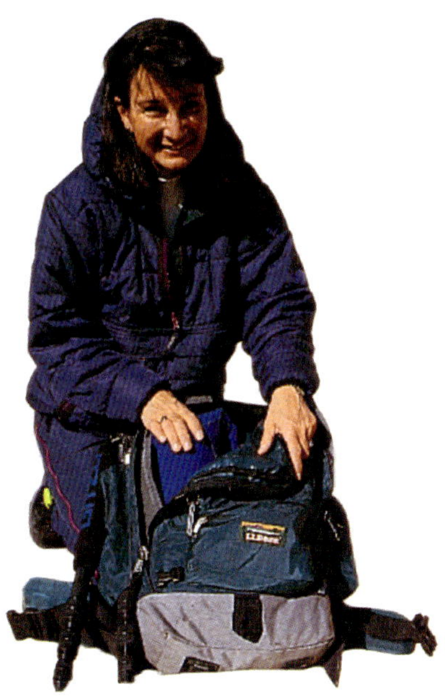

A well-designed and unassuming pack protects my equipment and provides a comfortable means of carrying it. Cut an inexpensive closed-cell foam pad with a sharp knife for extra padding. No one will guess the value of the pack's contents!

INNER PACK

2-3 Camera bodies	3 Film magazines
2 Extension tubes	Flash/Batteries
3 Filters	3 Lenses & shades
Tripod head	Light meter/batteries

OUTER ZIPPED POCKETS

Travel documents

◆

Tripod slides into space between outer side pocket and main pack.

◆

Accessories in a zippered plastic bag: duct tape, instruction manuals, extra trash bag,

bungy cord, emergency film

◆

Cable releases
Lens cleaning cloth
Screwdriver kit
Small flash, extra dark slide, business cards
Model release forms
Rubber bands for exposed film

FIRST AID KIT in a nylon stuff sack:

Bandaid bandages, prescription medicines, adhesive tape, water purifying tablets, cold/sinus/flu/upset stomach/diarrhea pills, aspirin, ibuprofen, nasal spray, eye ointment, blister medication, pocket knife, astringent, matches

PAGE	LOCATION	LENS
1.	Schoodic Peninsula, Maine	120mm
3.	Baxter State Park, Maine	50mm
	Yellowstone NP	140-280mm
4.	Yellowstone, Mud Volcano	120mm
	Image of JH courtesy Jim Progin	
6.	Alaska, Inside Passage	140-280mm
8.	Alaska, Inside Passage	140-280mm
10.	Riffelberg, Switzerland	120mm
	Two Top, West Yellowstone	140-280mm
	Beaver Creek, Colorado	120mm
11.	Kilimanjaro	120mm
	NYC Skyline, Bob Gallagher	250mm
	Beaver Creek Resort™	140-280mm
12.	Kilimanjaro summit	120mm
	Monhegan Island, Maine	250mm
	The Big Island, Hawaii	120 mm
13.	Camden, Maine	120mm, Proxar 0.5
	Vail Pass, CO	120mm/Metz40 MZ-2flash
	Yellowstone	120mm
14.	Glacier NP	120mm/500mm
	Denali NP Alaska	500mm (both)
	(1) Alaska	120mm lens 32mm Ext.
	(2) Inside Passage	120mm lens, Proxar 1.0
15.	Jackson, NH (May)	120mm, Proxar 1.0
	Wonder Lake, Denali NP	500mm
	Alaska, Inside Passage	30mm
16.	Monhegan Island, Maine	120mm
	Model	140-280mm/Metz flash
17.	Waterton Lakes NP	120mm
	Injured Model	500mm
	Courtesy Skip Cohen	500mm
18-19.	Tiger models	500mm
20.	Yellowstone	250mm/50mm

PAGE	LOCATION	LENS
21.	Antigua courtesy Bob Gallagher	38mm
22-23.	Meadows at Beaver Creek	
24.	Waterton Lakes, Canada	120mm
25.	Katmai NP, Alaska	
26.	Camp Denali, AK	250mm, 56mm
	Extension and 1.0 Proxar	
27.	Inside Passage, Alaska	30mm
28-29.	Bass Harbor, Maine	120mm
	Zermatt, Switzerland	250mm
	Tour du Mt. Blanc, France	80mm
30-31.	Wonder Lake, Denali	140-280mm
	Yellowstone	120mm/1.0 Proxar
32.	Pinkham Notch, NH	500mm
	Yellowstone	250mm
	Yellowstone	30mm
33.	Nugget Pond, Camp Denali	30mm
	Mt. Desert Island, Maine	120mm
	Yellowstone	120mm

PAGE	LOCATION	LENS
34.	Bar Harbor, Maine	120mm/1.0 Proxar
	Grand Tetons NP, WY	120mm, 0.5 Proxar
	Coast of Maine	120mm, 56 & 32mm Ext.
35.	Glacier NP	120mm, 56 & 32mm Ext. Softar II
	Denali NP	180mm/56mm Ext.
	Smokies NP	120 mm/32 Ext 1.0 Proxar
36.	The Smokies, Cades Cove	250mm
38.	Cape Churchill, Manitoba	500mm
39.	Inside Passage, AK	140-280mm
40.	Hayden Valley, Yellowstone	140-280mm
41.	Jordan Pond, Acadia NP	120mm
42.	Inside Passage, Alaska	180mm
	Mountain Lion Model	500mm
	Magdalen Islands, Quebec	38mm Biogon
43.	Brooks Lake Lodge WY	50mm
	Lauterbrunnen, Switzerland	120mm
	Injured Red Tail Hawk	500mm
44.	Acadia NP	120mm/8mm Ext., II Softar
45.	Matterhorn, Zermatt	500mm
	Glacier NP	120mm, 32mm Ext.
	Camp Denali	140-280 mm/Pano mask
	Velbon™ Macro Slider	120mm
	Acadia NP	120mm/1.0 & 0.5 Proxars
46.	Gulf of St. Lawrence	120mm
	Camp Denali/Labor Day	120mm
47.	Models, courtesy Skip Cohen	350mm
	Wengen, Switzerland	120mm
48.	Katmai NP, AK	120mm
	Monument Valley, AZ	50mm
	Camp Denali, AK	120mm
	Tenth Mountain Hut, CO	50mm
52.	Castle Geyser, Yellowstone	250mm

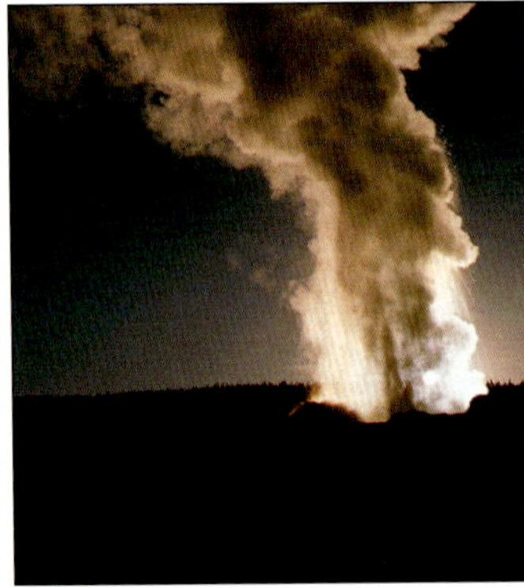

KODAK

For information on Kodak professional products, call 1-800-242-2424, ext. 19. For processing Kodak professional color films, call 1-800-242-2424, ext 60. Internet address: http://www.Kodak.com America On Line: Keyword Kodak, CompuServe: GO Kodak

HASSELBLAD

Hasselblad cameras and accessories are sold exclusively through Authorized Hasselblad Dealers. For a list in the United States, contact Hasselblad USA, Inc. 10 Madison Rd., Fairfield, NJ 07004. Telephone 1-201-227-7320 or fax 1-201-227-4216.

L.L. BEAN

Call L.L. Bean's special Sporting Goods Information Team, any day, 8 am to 10 pm at 1-800-221-4221, ext. 3100, to outfit yourself with clothing and gear for outdoor adventures. Visit us on the internet at http://www./llbean.com or write L.L. Bean Inc. Casco St., Freeport, ME 04033